A Parent's Guide to Empowering Children with Special Needs

101 Practical Tips to Help Your Child Thrive and Reach Their Full Potential

A Parent's Guide to Empowering Children with Special Needs

101 Practical Tips to Help Your Child Thrive and Reach Their Full Potential

Andrea Campbell

Pocket Learner Publishing

© Copyright Andrea Campbell 2023 - All rights reserved.

The content contained in this book may not be reproduced, duplicated or transmitted without direct written permission from the author or publisher.

Under no circumstances will any blame or legal responsibility be held against the publisher, or author, for any damages, reparation, or monetary loss due to the information contained within this book; either directly or indirectly. You are responsible for your own choices, actions, and results.

Legal Notice:

This book is copyright protected and is only for personal use. You cannot amend, distribute, sell, use, quote, or paraphrase any par, or the content within this book without the consent of the author or publisher.

Disclaimer Notice:

Please note that the information contained in this text is for educational and entertainment purposes only. All effort has been executed to present accurate, up-to-date, and reliable, complete information. No warranties of any kind are declared or implied. Readers acknowledge that the author is not engaging in rendering legal, financial, medical, or professional advice. The content within this book has been derived from various sources. Please consult a licensed professional before attempting any techniques outlined in this book.

By reading this document, the reader agrees that under no circumstances is the author responsible for any direct or indirect losses incurred as a result of the use of the information contained within this document, including, but not limited to - errors, omissions, or inaccuracies.

ISBN: (sc) 978-1-914997-37-2   (hc) 978-1-914997-38-9

I would like to thank Richmond and Shari for their inspiration, understanding, and patience.

This book is dedicated to families across the globe who are caring for children with special needs.

Keep shining your light so that they can shine theirs!

Table of Contents

Introduction 1
Chapter 1 7
Understanding Special Needs 7
    Special Needs – What is it? 7
    Causes of Special Needs... 12
    Other Types of Special Needs 13
    Symptoms of Special Needs.. 14
    Diagnosing Special Needs 16
    Treatment & Management of Special Needs 16
    Legal and Ethical Issues in Special Needs..................... 19
Chapter 2 25
Love and Acceptance... 25
Chapter 3 33
Education and Learning.. 33
Chapter 4 45
Independence and Life Skills 45
Chapter 5 52
Communication.. 52
Chapter 6 62
Socialization and Relationships 62
Chapter 7 70
Behaviour Management 70
Chapter 8 80

Emotional and Mental Health 80

Chapter 9 88

Physical Health and Mobility 88

Chapter 10 96

Technology and Adaptations 96

Chapter 11 102

Family Support 102

Chapter 12 110

Self-esteem and Personal Growth 110

Chapter 13 118

Community Involvement and Resources 118

Chapter 14 126

Supplementary Therapies 126

Conclusion 138

Resources 146

Introduction

Raising children with special needs can be a challenging and emotional journey for parents and families. It requires love, patience, and dedication to support the child's physical, emotional, mental, and social development.

One of the main challenges to parents, when their child has special needs, is accepting the child's diagnosis. As expectant parents, we dream of what they will be like and what they will do as they grow up. However, when your child is born with a disability, those dreams are significantly impacted, leaving you to rethink everything.

All children need patience, warmth, and compassion. They need to feel loved and connected. For that to happen, they need people to communicate with them and understand what they are saying. Children with special needs are no exception. In addition to the above needs, they may have physical, emotional, sensory, or learning needs that will demand more attention. The information in this book will show you that, despite the difficulties, with help and the appropriate support, your child can learn and achieve immeasurable feats, and the rewards of seeing the growth are extremely gratifying.

This guide provides practical advice and inspiration for parents and wider families of children with special needs. It covers various areas, including education and learning, communication, behavior management, physical health, mobility, and emotional and mental health. Additionally, it highlights the importance of family and community involvement in promoting our children's physical and emotional development.

While every child with special needs is unique and has individual requirements, this guide presents experiences and case studies that can boost aspirations and encourage all parents and families.

My Story

My daughter has Down Syndrome and is also on the Autism Spectrum. She requires additional care and attention, a tailored curriculum, and help with her self-care. Her academic learning is slow, but her understanding is sharp, and she is a clever, witty child. I realized early on that my life would change drastically as I became her caregiver and advocate.

Introduction

I've battled every step of the way to access resources, therapies, and care support. I've challenged government, school, religious, and community officials. We've spent many nights researching her diagnosis and learning about new developments in the field. Although never-ending, it is a fulfilling job—especially when our labor yields fruit and our child takes another step toward independence.

When I realized that my daughter was not progressing in her traditional educational institution, a conversation with her class teacher helped me understand that the school would be unable to give her the support she needed. I successfully lobbied for her to change schools.

My efforts to support her learning did not stop with this, however. I developed an educational resource to aid her learning. I call it the Pocket Learner because it entails placing cards into pockets. The Pocket Learner was so helpful that I decided to share it with the world, and it has earned various awards and accolades.

The Mission

Due to personal experience and involvement in parent groups, I have gathered vast experience in special needs parenting, and my understanding has grown in leaps and bounds. While I refuse to call myself an expert, I feel that my knowledge is helpful to parents who are on a similar journey and who, like me, sometimes find themselves groping in the dark or navigating choppy waters. You can find many experts with theoretical knowledge, but only a parent truly knows how it feels when everyone else is asleep, but your mind and heart are racing because you are up late, yet again, with care duties or preparing for the next doctor's visit.

Parenting through challenges that no one else can see, let alone understand, is incredibly lonely. Parents and caregivers of children with special needs often tread unfamiliar waters requiring extreme courage and perseverance. It does not help that our struggles often plague us in a lonely, uncelebrated realm from the public's view.

I share in this text what I have learned so that other families can eliminate or reduce the struggles and accompanying stress. This guide will help you feel more empowered and confident in providing your special child with optimum care and support. This is a relatively succinct text but if you are looking for more detail regarding how to care for your special child, I published two comprehensive books on the subject, I have listed on the back pages of this book. I hope the book will offer some solace and a sense of togetherness. You are not alone.

Throughout the text, I refer to the children as "special." That's not to say that other children aren't special or that this child is more special. This book focuses on how physical and cognitive impairments or challenges

Introduction

affect our children with special needs and how families can employ strategies to navigate their journey into a peaceful and happy existence.

The book contains case studies shared by parents on an online forum. Their names are fictitious, but their experiences are real and packed with lessons from this very special sector of society. As we endeavor to build a more inclusive and supportive world for people with disabilities, we must collaborate to ensure that every child can access the necessary resources and support to reach their full potential. Let us continue to advocate for our remarkable children and uplift them so their light can shine brightly in the world.

*If you don't have
what it takes,*

take what you have.

—Andrea Campbell

Chapter 1

Understanding Special Needs

"Understanding is the first step to acceptance, and only with acceptance can there be recovery"
—*J.K. Rowling*

Special Needs – What is it?

The term "special needs" refers to any disabilities or difficulties that cause a person to require additional services or support to access education, recreation, or other areas of life. People can be born with special needs, or they may develop in childhood or adulthood. Special needs is an umbrella term encompassing multiple conditions and challenges that generally fall into one of the following four groups:

i) Developmental – Children who are not developing intellectually, socially, or physically like children their age may have developmental needs due to genetic or environmental factors. Autism Spectrum Disorder (ASD) and Down Syndrome are common conditions in this group. Intellectual disability covers:

a) Intellectual functioning (learning, judgment, problem-solving, abstract thinking, memory, reasoning, and academic skills).

b) Adaptive functioning (the ability to function and take care of oneself independently, such as performing personal care tasks, managing money, and performing work, school, or home tasks);

c) Social functioning (the capability to function acceptably in society, using skills such as communication, social judgment, reading social cues, respecting social rules, making friends, and comprehending the consequences of one's actions).

The American Psychiatric Association reported that 1% of the population has an intellectual disability. Some 85% of these people have mild cases. Figures from Public Health England (2016) and population data from the Office for National Statistics (2020) estimate that 1.5 million people in the UK have an intellectual disability.

ASD is a neurodevelopmental condition that causes social, behavioral, and communication challenges. If you are autistic, it does not denote an illness or disease. Rather, it means your brain works differently from other people's. It is unclear what causes autism; however, genetic and environmental factors are suspected. People who are autistic may be unable to make or sustain eye contact, and they may lack interest in social interactions. In addition, they may use non-verbal communication and have sensory sensitivities.

Please note that autism is a spectrum that affects people differently. Some people need little or no support, while others may require assistance daily. As discussed, autism in itself is not regarded as a special need, but some people who are autistic may also have special needs. A child who is both on the autistic spectrum and has co-occurring special needs will likely present differently, learn differently, and require different individual supports than an autistic child who does not have co-occurring special needs.

According to UK National Health Service 2021 statistics, the percentage of people with a learning disability diagnosed with autism is increasing steadily each year.

Down syndrome is a common form of special needs. People with the condition have an extra chromosome that changes brain and body development. They typically have distinct physical features, including a flatter nose, smaller ears, hands, and feet, a short neck, and almond-shaped eyes. They usually have lower-than-average IQs and experience developmental delays.

Learning disabilities fall within this group. The term applies when the person needs additional support in order to access education. They may experience difficulty expressing thoughts in written form, reading, math, or processing information. Some common learning disabilities include Dysgraphia (difficulty writing), Dyslexia (difficulty reading), Auditory Processing Disorder (the brain has difficulty receiving and interpreting sounds), Visual Processing Disorder (issues with how the brain processes visual information and Dyscalulia (problems with numbers and math).

ii) Behavioural/Emotional – Behavioral or mental health special needs can affect the child's ability to form and sustain healthy relationships, sit still in a learning or social setting, or appropriately respond to disciplinary measures. Examples of behavioral and mental health special needs are ADHD (inattentiveness, often combined with hyperactivity), anxiety, oppositional defiant disorder (moodiness, disobedience), obsessive-compulsive disorder, dissociation, post-traumatic stress disorder, anxiety, depression, bipolar, and eating disorders such as anorexia, bulimia, and others.

iii) Physical/Medical – Children with medical needs frequently visit doctors and hospitals as their parents seek medical care. These conditions include cerebral palsy (brain damage that affects movement, motor skills, and muscle), muscular dystrophy (diseases that weaken and break down skeletal muscle), multiple sclerosis, juvenile arthritis, leukemia, epilepsy, allergies, and asthma.

iv) Sensory Impaired – Sensory impairment includes any type of difficulty that an individual has with one of their five senses. When a person experiences loss of a sensory function, the way they interact with the environment is affected. Sensory impairment includes blindness, hearing loss or deafness, and kinesthetic impairments, such as peripheral neuropathy, which affect the ability to feel sensations.

It is clear, therefore, that "special needs" covers a wide range of impairments. Many people can read and write, use telephones and computers, make decisions, hold jobs, maintain relationships, live independently, and interact in their communities. Others need significant support for personal care and to access and participate in their communities. Unfortunately, people with special needs across the globe continue to face challenges such as exclusion, oppression, ridicule, and victimization. Such experiences contribute to secondary issues such as depression, anxiety, and other physical health problems.

Causes of Special Needs

In many cases, the precise cause of special needs is unknown. Special needs can have several causes, including genetic abnormalities, injuries, impairments from diseases such as meningitis, and developmental disabilities. However, some children will never have a specific cause identified for their special needs.

Any condition that impacts the brain and begins before the age of 18, including before birth, can cause special needs. However, special needs can also develop later in childhood or adolescence due to conditions that cause brain damage. Many factors can impair brain development, some of which I have listed below.

Genetic conditions - Many genetic diseases are related to special needs. For example, some conditions can be abnormal genes inherited from parents or errors that occur when genes combine. Common genetic disorders include Down syndrome, fragile X syndrome, and phenylketonuria (PKU).

Complications during pregnancy - The use of alcohol or other drugs during pregnancy can cause special needs. In this case, the brain does not develop properly before birth.

Environmental factors - Other risk factors that can harm brain development include ecological contaminants, malnutrition, and illnesses. One example of an environmental factor is lead poisoning. Young children sometimes eat paint that has flaked off the walls of their home, and paint often contains lead which has harmful effects on growing children, including damage to the brain.

Problems at birth - Premature infants and those with low birth weights are most often at significant risk of special needs. Unusual stress on the head during delivery, lack of oxygen or other problems during birth can also cause the condition.

Childhood illnesses - The absence of adequate nutrition or diseases such as whooping cough, chicken pox, and measles can lead to meningitis and encephalitis, damaging a growing child's brain. Childhood injuries can also lead to special needs. A head blow or a violent shaking may cause brain damage and special needs.

Other Types of Special Needs

As discussed, there are some conditions typically classified as special needs. I have outlined some of these conditions above, but it is important to mention the following conditions, which are common but less well-known.

Fragile X syndrome – a common type of inherited special needs, is a genetic condition caused by a mutation in the X chromosome. Its symptoms include speech problems, sensory issues, and behavioral changes.

Prader-Willi syndrome (PWS) – a rare genetic condition affecting the mental as well as physical development of a child. A feature of this disorder is hyperphagia (or chronic eating) which often leads to obesity. Other symptoms include challenging behavior, weak muscle tone, and intellectual delays.

Fetal alcohol spectrum disorders (FASDs) - refer to a range of conditions brought about by alcohol abuse while pregnant. Common symptoms of FASDs include visual or hearing problems, abnormal facial features, lower IQ, and cognitive difficulties.

Symptoms of Special Needs

Children who appear physically neurotypical could also have special needs, which may not be revealed until they begin to have difficulty with schoolwork. Children with special needs might exhibit symptoms earlier than those with a milder form. Here are some of the early signs:
− Communicating using nonverbal means, such as expressions and gestures
− Delayed motor skills
− Missing developmental milestones
− Difficulty focusing and controlling impulses
− Difficulty making eye contact and responsiveness
− Difficulty expressing needs and emotions

- Difficulty learning from experience
- Difficulty planning or following schedules or routines
- Difficulty regulating emotions and behavior
- Difficulty remembering things
- Difficulty making friends
- lack of ability to engage in conversation
- difficulty following instructions
- trouble with fine motor skills
- Difficulty solving problems, thinking logically, or thinking in an abstract way
- Difficulty speaking or reading
- Difficulty understanding processes such as the requirement to pay for things, the significance of time, or how to use a phone
- Difficulty understanding the concept of the consequences of their actions
- Limited functioning in daily activities
- Reaching developmental milestones later than usual
- Reduced judgment and decision-making skills
- Needing help with feeding
- Needing help with personal care and getting dressed
- A reduced ability to complete household tasks
- Seizures
- Struggling to develop social skills and understand social rules or cues
- Temper tantrums
- Trouble following simple instructions.

The symptoms of special needs vary depending on the type and severity of special needs or the disability a child has. Developmental special needs are usually apparent early in life, but some aren't observed until later.

Diagnosing Special Needs

To diagnose special needs, doctors perform several tests to assess the person's intellectual and adaptive functioning. These tests may include:
- An IQ test
- Interviews with individuals and others who have observed the person's adaptive functioning—their conceptual, social, and practical functioning. These interviews may be conducted with family members or teachers
- Assessing if someone has the skills necessary to live independently
- General medical tests
- Neurological and psychological tests
- Special education tests
- Hearing, speech, and vision tests
- Physical therapy evaluations.

Treatment & Management of Special Needs

Treatment for children with special needs depends on the type of special need or disability and its severity. Some children will need ongoing courses of medicine; others will need therapies or a combination of both.

Early intervention is important, and parents must seek help from healthcare professionals or specialists as soon as possible to help their children.

There is a wide range of therapies for children with special needs. Below are some key therapies that may be useful in promoting your child's development, education, interests, and personal well-being.

Speech therapy - to help with any speech or language problems. Speech therapy involves working with individuals to improve their communication skills. It can benefit individuals with special needs who may struggle with language and communication. In addition, speech therapy can help children with special needs develop communication skills. Parents should work with their child's healthcare team to determine if speech therapy is needed and, if so, to figure out how to incorporate it into their child's care plan.

Occupational therapy - to develop strategies for everyday living, focusing on activities such as dressing, bathing, and using the bathroom. Occupational therapy involves working with individuals to improve their ability to perform daily activities. It can benefit individuals with special needs by enhancing their independence and overall quality of life.

Physical therapy/physiotherapy - to improve balance, hand-eye coordination, motor skills, walking, and muscle stretching. Traditionally, it has been thought that physiotherapists use a more holistic approach to treatment, relying on various modalities and manual therapy. At the same time, physical therapists employ an exercise-based approach with more exercise routines and stretches. This can benefit individuals with special needs who may have motor impairments or difficulty with coordination.

Behavioral therapy - to help with social and emotional development, such as controlling anger/aggression, appropriate public behavior, socialization, and forming peer relationships. Behavioral therapy involves working with individuals to modify their behavior and develop new skills. It can be helpful for individuals with special needs who may have difficulty with communication, socialization, and adaptive behavior.

Treatment may also include family therapy. Family therapy aims to help family members understand the nature of special needs. It also helps them develop skills for dealing with their child's special needs. Parents may also receive counseling to help them deal with anger or guilt.

You can engage in a range of other therapies to empower your child. I have listed some of them in chapter 14 of this book. The type of therapy that each child needs will differ. A qualified therapist or practitioner can help to ascertain the treatment that may be appropriate for your child. Additionally, consider your child's preferences and interests when selecting the therapies, as they may be more motivated and engaged if they enjoy the chosen activity.

Legal and Ethical Issues in Special Needs

Legal and ethical issues in special needs arise in various contexts, including education, employment, healthcare, and community living. Legal and ethical issues in special needs highlight the need for greater awareness, understanding, and support for people with special needs and their families. Advocacy and policy efforts are needed to promote the rights and well-being of individuals with special needs in all domains of life. Some of the legal and ethical issues in this domain are discussed below:

Discrimination - Individuals with special needs are often subjected to discrimination and exclusion in various domains, such as education, employment, and housing. Legal protections, such as the Americans with Disabilities Act (ADA) and the Individuals with Disabilities Education Act (IDEA), aim to prevent discrimination and ensure equal opportunities for people with disabilities.

Informed consent - Individuals with special needs may have difficulty understanding and making informed decisions about their healthcare and treatment options. Healthcare providers must ensure that people with special needs receive appropriate support and accommodations to make informed decisions about their healthcare.

Guardianship and autonomy - Guardianship is a legal arrangement in which someone is appointed as a decision-maker for a person with special needs. However, guardianship can also limit the autonomy and self-determination of those with special needs. There is a need to balance the requirement for protection and support with the right to make decisions and exercise autonomy.

Community living - Many people with special needs require support and assistance with daily living activities. Community living arrangements, such as supported living arrangements and group homes, aim to provide people with special needs the support they need to live independently and participate in their communities. However, the quality and availability of these services are of concern.

Reproductive rights - People with special needs can make decisions about their reproductive health, including contraception, pregnancy, and parenting. However, access to information and support for those with special needs in this area remains a concern.

Education - People with special needs have the right to access appropriate education for their needs and abilities. The IDEA provides legal protections for individuals with disabilities in the educational context, including providing accommodations and support services.

Employment - Individuals with special needs face significant barriers to employment, including discrimination and limited job opportunities. The ADA provides legal protections for employees with disabilities, including reasonable accommodations. However, employers need greater awareness and support to promote the inclusion of employees with special needs in the workforce.

Healthcare - Individuals with special needs may face barriers when accessing healthcare, including inadequate communication and lack of understanding by healthcare providers. Healthcare providers must have appropriate training and support to ensure that people with special needs have access to high-quality and suitable healthcare.

Abuse and neglect - People with special needs are at greater risk of abuse and neglect, including physical, sexual, and emotional abuse. Society must recognize and address this issue, and legal and ethical frameworks must protect those with special needs from abuse and neglect.

Research ethics - Research involving individuals with special needs raises unique ethical concerns, including issues related to informed consent, vulnerability, and exploitation. Researchers must adhere to high ethical standards in research involving people with special needs. In addition, they must ensure that the rights and well-being of participants are protected.

Assistive technology - People with special needs may benefit from using assistive technology to support their communication, mobility, and daily living activities. Assistive technology is not readily available, and there is a constant need for appropriate training and support for those with special needs in using this technology.

Access to justice - Individuals with special needs may encounter barriers when accessing the justice system, including difficulties communicating with lawyers and understanding legal processes. The justice system must provide appropriate accommodations and support to ensure that people with special needs have equal access to justice.

Stigma and social attitudes - People with special needs may face stigma and discrimination from society, limiting their opportunities and affecting their well-being. Society must promote positive attitudes and acceptance of those with special needs and recognize and value their contribution to the community.

International human rights - People with special needs have the same human rights as everyone, as recognized by international human rights frameworks such as the United Nations Convention on the Rights of Persons with Disabilities. Society must recognize and uphold the human rights of people with special needs and work towards greater inclusion and equality for all people, regardless of ability.

End-of-life care - Individuals with special needs may have unique needs and preferences regarding end-of-life care. Healthcare providers must provide appropriate support and accommodations to ensure that people with special needs receive high-quality end-of-life care that meets their needs and wishes.

Legal and ethical issues in special needs are diverse, complex, and multifaceted and require a comprehensive approach that addresses the unique needs and challenges those with special needs face. They highlight the need for greater awareness, understanding, and support for people with special needs and their loved ones, as well as advocacy and policy efforts to promote the rights and well-being of people with special needs in all domains of life and to ensure that they have equal opportunities and access to high-quality services and support.

Trees bear fruit, fruits have seeds, seeds hold trees.

Everyone, indeed everything

has something to offer in the cycle of life.

—Andrea Campbell

Chapter 2

Love and Acceptance

"Love is acceptance – accepting people as they are. Just acceptance and caring"
—*Louise Hay*

One of the most important aspects of caring for a child with special needs is ensuring the child knows they are loved and accepted for who they are. As a parent, you must provide unconditional love and acceptance to your child, irrespective of their abilities or disabilities.

When you show your children you love and accept them, you give them the confidence and security they need to thrive. This will help them build a positive sense of self-worth, self-esteem, and self-confidence which they will carry with them throughout their lives.

In addition, children with special needs often face unique challenges in life, such as difficulty with learning and communication, social isolation, and discrimination. As a result, they may feel different or isolated from their peers and struggle to navigate the world around them.

Showing love and acceptance to your special child helps combat the negative attitudes and discrimination they may face from others. In addition, by providing a safe and loving environment at home, you can help your child feel valued and accepted in a world that may not always embrace their differences.

Although my daughter is unable to hold a conversation, I hug her every morning as she leaves for school and tell her that she is beautiful. I kiss her face, stroke her hair and prompt her to repeat the words: "I am beautiful." I feel that these actions make her feel loved and valued, and they boost her confidence. She goes to school knowing that her mom loves her and that she is beautiful.

Love and acceptance are powerful tools for building a solid and positive relationship with your child. When you show them love, you create a bond of trust and respect that will help you to provide them with the support and guidance they need to learn and grow. This bond will also help to foster open communication, which is critical for understanding your child's needs and feelings.

A loving environment gives a child with special needs the support and security they need to thrive and build positive relationships. It is essential to promote their emotional, psychological, and social well-being and build a strong and positive relationship between parent and child. Here are some ways that you can show love and support to your child:

1. **Understanding**: Try to understand your child's disability and how it affects their life. This may entail researching their diagnosis or attending short courses to understand the condition. This will help you to better communicate with your child, anticipate their needs, and provide appropriate support. As time progresses, you will better understand your child, and professionals will rely on your experience with your child as they administer treatments and therapies.

2. **Patience**: Children with special needs may need more time to process information or complete tasks, so patience is essential. Spend time working with your child and celebrate their progress, no matter how small. Once you understand that your child may struggle with certain tasks or behaviors, you'll be prepared to wait, allow them the time they need to complete tasks, and avoid rushing or pressuring them.

3. **Affection**: Hug your child, say "I love you," and show them physical affection often. Tell them

how wonderful and clever they are. Remember, anything that you feed will grow. Therefore, feed their self-esteem and nurture them so they grow in confidence. This confidence will empower them to take on and overcome the challenges and setbacks they inevitably will face as they navigate life. Provide encouragement and positive reinforcement, celebrate their strengths and accomplishments, and help them overcome obstacles.

4. **Attention**: This involves being present and attentive when your child speaks and asking open-ended questions to encourage conversation. For example: What makes you happy? Why does it make you happy? What did you do at school? If your child is non-verbal, find a way to communicate with them, perhaps using signs or an established communication system. The fact that your child doesn't use speech does not mean that they have nothing to say!

    Listen to your child without judgment and respond in a way that shows you understand and care about what they are saying. In listening, practice empathy, try to see the world from your child's perspective, and understand their feelings, thoughts, and behavior. Practicing active listening and providing opportunities for your child to share their thoughts and feelings can strengthen your bond and boost their communication skills.

5. **Independence Fostering**: Encourage your child to participate in household chores and tasks to develop independence skills. This can include setting the table, folding laundry, or washing dishes. Build a solid and supportive relationship with your child by spending quality time with them, engaging in activities they enjoy, and being an active participant in their lives. Help them develop independence in daily living skills such as dressing, grooming, and cooking. This can be done by gradually teaching your child how to do these tasks independently and providing the necessary tools and resources.

Children with special needs can be a source of joy and happiness for their parents. We learn to recognize and acknowledge the small things in life and celebrate our children's tiniest accomplishments. These attitudes may baffle parents of neurotypical children who take these feats for granted.

Despite the challenges of parenting a child with special needs, parents must love and care for their special child just as they would any other child. Only when love is unconditional can you look beyond the difficulties and start to find joy in your unique parental role.

A Parent's Guide to Empowering Children with Special Needs

Case Study

Mrs. Leeson is a 45-year-old mother of two children. Her younger child, Tommy, was born with special needs. Mrs. Leeson was devastated when she learned about Tommy's condition and struggled to accept it. She couldn't understand why this had happened to her family, and as a smoker, she often blamed herself for Tommy's disability.

As Tommy grew older, Mrs. Leeson faced many challenges in raising him. She found it hard to communicate with him and often felt frustrated when he didn't respond to her. She was also worried about Tommy's future and his ability to live independently.

Mrs. Leeson's journey toward accepting and loving her disabled child was slow and gradual. She began by educating herself about Tommy's condition and how she could help him. She read books, attended workshops, and spoke to other parents of children with disabilities. She learned about the importance of early intervention and started working with therapists to develop Tommy's skills.

As Mrs. Leeson began to see Tommy's progress, her attitude toward him changed. She began to appreciate his unique qualities and started seeing him as an individual with strengths and weaknesses. She also realized that Tommy's disability was not her fault and that she couldn't have prevented it.

Over time, Mrs. Leeson's relationship with Tommy improved. She started communicating with him more effectively and found ways to connect with him. She also started to involve Tommy in family activities and social events. As a result, Tommy started to become more independent and confident.

The turning point in Mrs. Leeson's journey came when she attended a special needs conference. There, she met other parents and caregivers of children with disabilities and heard their stories. She realized she was not alone in her struggles and that a whole community of people understood what she was going through. Mrs. Leeson also met adults with special needs who were living fulfilling lives. She saw that Tommy could have a bright future and that his disability didn't have to define him. This experience gave Mrs. Leeson a newfound sense of hope and motivation.

Today, Mrs. Leeson has fully accepted and loves her child. She sees Tommy as a unique individual with talents and abilities. She supports him in pursuing his interests and goals and celebrates his achievements. Mrs. Leeson also advocates for the rights of people with disabilities and is involved in community organizations that support them.

Mrs. Leeson's journey towards accepting and loving her child was long and challenging. It required patience, perseverance, and a willingness to learn and grow. But in the end, Mrs. Leeson's journey was also rewarding. She learned to appreciate the small things in life, developed a deeper understanding of herself and others, and became a stronger and more compassionate person.

Chapter 3

Education and Learning

"Children have to be educated, but they have also to be left to educate themselves."
—*Ernest Dimnet*

Parents play a crucial role in promoting education and learning in their children. A research paper from the International Journal of Humanities and Social Science entitled "Role of Parents in Training of Children with Special Needs" concluded: "Parents play a vital role in the training and development of children with special needs. In training functional skills among children with disabilities, parents help a lot in achieving target goals. They are considered leading mentors for children in their early and later life."

When my child was in primary school, she exhibited extremely challenging behavior, adversely affecting her learning. Her teachers could not relate effectively to her, and she had to leave the mainstream school by the age of 10. I embarked on a mission to help her learn. While working with her, I developed a set of resources called the Pocket Learner. The resources helped her build her vocabulary, learn to read and count. Importantly, they helped to develop her focus and increased her attention. Those resources are now being shared with families across the globe.

Once we acknowledge that our children have special needs and learn to accept them as they are, we will be better able to help them learn and grow. With a positive mindset about our children's capability, we do what it takes to help them achieve their potential.

There are many processes in which parents can be involved, including identification, assessment, educational programming, training, teaching, and evaluation. Here are some strategies that can help:

6. **Early intervention**: Early intervention is crucial for children with special needs. You should seek interventions such as special education services, occupational therapy, and speech therapy as soon as possible. The earlier your child receives interventions, the better the outcomes will likely be.

Education and Learning

7. **Creating a supportive learning environment**: Children with special needs may struggle in a traditional classroom setting. Create a calm and predictable home environment to reduce stress and foster a sense of security. This involves establishing routines and structure, providing a quiet and comfortable space for your child, and minimizing sensory overload.

   To reduce anxiety and stress, create an environment without sudden changes or surprises. This can include using a visual schedule, providing advance notice of changes, and creating a quiet space for your child to relax. Provide necessary resources, including books, educational toys, pictures, charts, and visual schedules to help your child understand and process new information. This can make learning more accessible and engaging for them.

8. **Multi-sensory approach**: Children with special needs often learn best through a multi-sensory approach that engages all of their senses. You can use games, music, and other interactive activities to help your child learn and consolidate information.

   Sensory play activities can help children with special needs develop their sensory processing skills. It can also provide opportunities for exploration and creativity, which are essential for their development. Create a sensory schedule with activities and techniques to help your child regulate sensory input and manage sensory issues. This can include activities such as sensory bins, weighted blankets, or sensory swings.

Providing opportunities for sensory stimulation, such as exploring textures or playing with sensory toys, can promote sensory integration. This can improve your child's ability to regulate their emotions and behaviors, help them better understand their surroundings, and improve their ability to process sensory information. Providing opportunities for your child to explore different textures, smells, and tastes can help develop their sensory processing skills. This can involve activities such as cooking or gardening.

9. **Incorporation of real-life experiences:** When you incorporate real-life experiences into your child's education, you help them understand concepts and apply them in practical situations. For example, consider taking your child to the grocery store and having them scan items and pay for them or select different fruits and vegetables. You could also consider allowing them to choose and pay for their favorite treats.

10. **Teaching problem-solving skills:** Encourage your child to problem-solve by asking questions and helping them generate solutions. For example, ask, "What should we do to solve this

problem?" When giving instructions to your child, provide clear and concise explanations to help them understand your expectations. This can help your child feel more independent and confident in completing tasks. Teaching your child social problem-solving strategies can help them navigate social situations and conflicts. This can involve teaching them to identify the problem, brainstorm solutions, evaluate their effectiveness, and implement the best solution.

Practicing problem-solving strategies using real-life scenarios and role-playing helps children develop critical thinking skills and build confidence in their problem-solving ability. If you practice problem-solving skills as a family, you will also promote teamwork. Therefore, it is an excellent idea to encourage everyone to participate and work together to solve problems.

11. **Peer Modeling:** When children with special needs see their peers successfully performing a task or behavior, it can increase their confidence and motivation to try it themselves. Peer modeling can also provide a more relatable and understandable example for your child, as their peers may share similar experiences and challenges. This may help reduce feelings of isolation and promote a sense of belonging. For example, if your child struggles to use a new assistive technology device, observing a peer

successfully using the same device may assist them in learning.

Peer modeling can also teach social skills like communication and friendship building. Observing their peers engaging in positive social interactions can help your child better understand social norms and improve their social skills.

12. **Peer Mentoring:** Peer mentoring can be a powerful tool for individuals with special needs to gain support and guidance from someone with similar experiences and can provide mentorship from a place of understanding.

Peer mentoring involves matching individuals with special needs with a peer mentor with similar experiences who can offer support and guidance. It has proved valuable to individuals with special needs in boosting their confidence and improving social skills. A peer mentor can help your child gain confidence in their abilities and feel more empowered to navigate challenges and achieve their goals. The process can help them develop their social and problem-solving skills by learning from their mentor's social interactions and modeling their behavior.

Both peer mentoring and peer modeling are great ways to teach new skills and behaviors and promote social inclusion and engagement. They

Education and Learning

are valuable tools for children with special needs to gain support, guidance, and mentorship from someone who understands their experiences and can provide personalized support.

13. **Vocational training and community service:** Vocational training can help your child prepare for future employment and promote independence. This can involve job shadowing, internships, or vocational education programs. Becoming involved in community service activities can help your child develop social skills, empathy, and a sense of purpose. You can look for local volunteer opportunities or organize your service projects.

14. **Transition planning:** Transitions can be challenging for children with special needs, but careful planning and preparation can make them smoother and more successful. Developing an effective transition plan involves working with your child, their teachers or support staff, and other professionals involved in their care. The plan should identify the goals for the transition, the steps to be taken, and who is responsible for each step. It should also take into account any accommodations or modifications that your child may need to be successful. This could include additional support, training, assistive technology, or environmental changes.

Transitions may include moving from school to work or from home to a center. A transition plan identifies potential challenges and solutions and involves your child. Planning and involving your child in the process can make them feel more ready and confident in the face of change. For example, you could use social stories to prepare your child for transitions, such as changing schools or starting a new activity. This can help them manage to their expectations and feel more comfortable with the change.

15. **Advocacy:** You should advocate for your child and ensure they receive appropriate services, education, and opportunities. This may include working with schools, doctors, and other professionals to help you meet your child's needs. You should defend your child's rights and advocate for their needs and interests in all areas.

Communicate regularly with your child's teachers to ensure they receive the support and accommodations they need to succeed. Attend parent-teacher meetings, and ask about your child's progress and any challenges they may face. Cooperate with the teachers to develop a plan to address areas where your child may need additional support. Always be bold and seek clarifications or pursue courses of action, uncomfortable though they may be.

Although you must advocate for your child, teaching them to advocate for themselves is important too. Teaching your child self-advocacy skills, such as communicating their needs and preferences to others, can promote independence and self-determination. It can also allow your child to feel more confident.

As with any neurotypical child, education, and learning are vital for children with special needs. They help the children develop independence, improve their social skills, build self-esteem, and boost their life chances. The ability to learn and grow is key to enhancing the quality of life of any child.

Promoting education and learning in children with special needs requires a collaborative effort between parents, educators, and other professionals. By creating a supportive learning environment, using a multi-sensory approach, incorporating real-life experiences, building social skills, and celebrating achievements, parents can assist their children in reaching their full potential.

Case Study

Meet Andrew, an 8-year-old boy with Down syndrome. Andrew loves to play with his toy cars. However, his parents have noticed that Andrew struggles with his schoolwork, particularly his reading and writing skills.

Andrew's parents decided to take action and help him with his education. They began by researching different teaching methods for children with Down syndrome and found that visual aids and hands-on activities can effectively improve their learning. They also sought the help of a special education teacher who specializes in teaching children with special needs. The teacher worked closely with Andrew and his parents to create an individualized education plan (IEP) that suited Andrew's needs and abilities.

Andrew's parents made sure to create a home environment conducive to learning. They designated a quiet study area for Andrew and provided him with educational materials, such as books with large print and colorful pictures and educational toys and games. His parents incorporated his interests into his studies to make learning fun for Andrew. For example, they used his toy cars to help him learn basic math skills like counting and sorting.

Andrew's parents also communicated regularly with his teachers and other professionals involved in his education. They attended parent-teacher conferences and sought feedback on his progress.

Andrew's reading skills have improved significantly with support and guidance from his parents and educators. He still has issues with writing but has weekly sessions with his school's occupational therapist to address his fine motor issues and help him with writing. Andrew is now doing better at school.

In summary, Andrew's parents were able to promote education and learning in their child by taking the following steps:

- Researching different teaching methods for children with special needs
- Working with a special education teacher to create an individualized education plan (IEP)
- Creating a home environment conducive to learning
- Incorporating his interests into his studies
- Communicating regularly with his teachers and other professionals involved in his education
- Requesting support from an occupational therapist at school.

What we earn gives us a living,

but it is what we learn that gives us a life.

—Andrea Campbell

Chapter 4

Independence and Life Skills

"It is easier to build strong children than to repair broken men"
—*Frederick Douglass*

Encouraging independence and self-reliance in a child with special needs is vital for their overall development and well-being. It helps children develop a sense of autonomy, self-esteem, and confidence, which lead to an improved quality of life. Let your child make decisions, and allow them to learn from their mistakes.

Our local government department awarded us care support for a few hours per week. The caregiver visits our home three evenings per week and carries out various activities with our daughter. These activities include dancing, trampolining, walking, academic work, playing, and cooking. Our daughter chooses the activities and the rewards when necessary. Sometimes she's had enough and refuses to engage, choosing instead to listen to her preferred music. Though we encourage her, we do not force her because if she has no interest in an activity, it shows in her behavior. So by following her cues and allowing her to choose, we achieve a win-win outcome.

Providing appropriate support and opportunities to learn and practice new skills is vital to promote your child's independence and self-reliance. This can occur through a variety of approaches, including:

16. **Empowerment**: Parents should empower their children to make independent decisions. This is particularly important when your special child is growing up with siblings. You should treat the children equally so the neuro-typical child is not busy with chores while the special child looks on. When you treat them alike, your special child will have a sense of normalcy and will develop an understanding of normal societal expectations. This strategy will also help build their social and interpersonal skills.

17. **Realistic goal setting:** It is necessary to set achievable goals for the child based on their abilities and interests. This can help them experience a sense of accomplishment and build self-confidence. You could start with small tasks

Education and Learning

to complete independently, such as dressing themselves, making their bed, or putting away toys. When they achieve their goals, it helps them build confidence and self-esteem. Be realistic about your child's capability, and avoid putting too much pressure on them.

18. **Structured routines:** A predictable routine can help a child with special needs feel more secure and in control. Clear instructions and routines can help your child develop independence and learn new skills. Use visual schedules where possible, to help your child understand and follow routines. This approach can help reduce anxiety and increase their sense of control and independence.

19. **Choices:** Allowing the child to make small choices inspires a spirit of being in control and builds their decision-making skills. Foster independence in decision-making by involving your child in making choices about their daily routines and activities. This can involve allowing them to take responsibility for their own life decisions, such as choosing their clothes or deciding their education and career path. Provide opportunities for making choices about their daily activities, such as what to wear or have for breakfast.

20. **Life skills:** Teaching your child basic life skills, such as personal hygiene, cooking, cleaning, and

laundry, helps them to become more self-sufficient and independent. In addition, use adaptive equipment such as specialized utensils or mobility aids to promote independence in daily living activities. This can include specialized utensils for eating, mobility aids such as walkers or wheelchairs, or even technology such as speech-generating devices. These tools allow your child to participate in activities and tasks that might otherwise be inaccessible, and their presence promotes independence and self-esteem.

21. **Technology:** Use smart home devices, reminder apps, or communication aids to support your child's independence and daily living skills. Furthermore, you can use assistive technology such as text-to-speech or digital organizers to promote your child's learning and growth.

22. **Positive reinforcement:** Praising and rewarding the child for their efforts and achievements can help to reinforce positive behavior and encourage them to continue developing their skills and independence.

Every child should be encouraged to learn life skills, regardless of their cognitive ability. Participating in their life increases their confidence, promotes independence, enhances their social skills, and prepares them for adulthood.

Education and Learning

Promoting independence and self-reliance in any child requires a supportive and structured environment and a willingness to adapt and modify teaching methods to meet the child's individual needs and abilities.

Supporting a child to build independence takes time and patience, but in so doing, you empower your child to develop the skills they need to succeed and thrive.

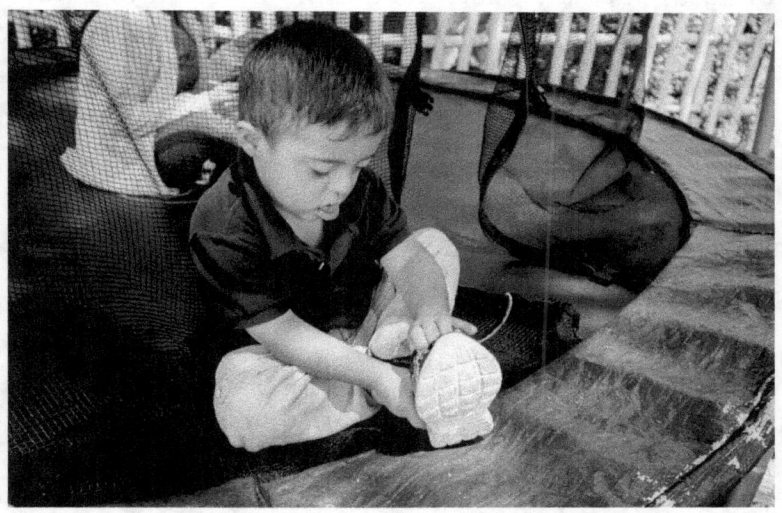

Case Study

Sophie is a 12-year-old girl with special needs. Her parents have been working to promote her independence and life skills to help her become more self-sufficient and confident.

To promote Sophie's independence, her parents started by identifying her strengths and interests.

They found that Sophie was particularly interested in cooking and baking, so they encouraged her to participate in meal planning and preparation. They worked together to create a structured routine, where Sophie would help plan the meals for the week and actively prepare the ingredients.

Sophie's parents also worked with her to develop her daily living skills, such as getting dressed, brushing her teeth, and doing her hair. They provided her with clear, step-by-step instructions and demonstrated each task until she could complete them independently. They also worked on time management skills, such as setting and sticking to a schedule. To reinforce these skills, Sophie's parents provided positive feedback when she completed a task independently. They also encouraged her to practice these skills in various settings, such as at home, school, and the community.

Over time, Sophie's independence and life skills improved, and she grew in confidence. Her parents continued to provide support and guidance but gradually stepped back to allow Sophie to take on more responsibility.

Sophie's parents' focus on promoting her strengths and interests, developing her daily living skills, and providing positive feedback and encouragement helped promote her independence and life skills. Giving her the support she needed to become more self-sufficient improved her overall well-being and quality of life.

Chapter 5

Communication

"The most important thing in communication is to hear what isn't being said"
—*Peter Drucker*

Building communication skills is integral to helping children with special needs succeed. Communication is a fundamental human right. Even though many of these children do not communicate using written, spoken, or sign language, they still communicate. This can include eye contact, gestures, facial expressions, body language, and contact, sounds like laughing or sighing, or using pictures and symbols.

Multi-modal communication is an approach that involves using a variety of communication methods to support individuals with special needs in expressing themselves and understanding others. This technique presents multiple options for self-expression and for understanding and using verbal, visual, and tactile communication. Multi-modal communication can help children better understand information and instructtions. Enhanced communication skills help individuals communicate their needs and desires more effectively, leading to improved comprehension, better social interaction, and greater independence and autonomy.

My daughter is learning sign language at school. They use signs and spoken and written words to communicate with the children in the classroom. At home, we use cards, video, audio, and gestures to communicate with her. Acknowledging and developing an understanding of how your child communicates and interpreting and responding are essential. Below are strategies you can use to promote your child's communication skills:

23. **Effective communication:** Great communication is essential for building a solid bond with your child. Ensure you communicate using pictures, gestures, or other nonverbal communication. Listen actively to your child and respond in a supportive and respectful way. To model good communication skills, you must use appropriate tone, inflection, and body language. Demonstrate how to ask questions, make requests, and respond to others. Model positive behavior because your child will practice what they observe, not necessarily what you tell them to do.

24. **Simple language:** Use concise language when communicating with your child. Speak slowly and clearly, and use short sentences that are easy to understand. Providing clear and concise instructtions can help your child understand your expectations and increase their ability to follow through on tasks. This can also help reduce frustration and improve their sense of accomplishment.

    Start with single-step instructions, for example:
    "Come here, please." You may want to add a second step later, such as:
    "Please come here and bring a cup for me." Then, when they are ready, you can say,
    "Please take a cup from the kitchen, fill it with water, and take it to your dad."
    This latter sentence is immensely more complex than the earlier ones and can be made more complex such as:
    "Please take a blue cup from the kitchen, fill it up to half with water, and bring it to your dad in the garage."
    A sentence like this would frustrate your child, and they may struggle to achieve it.

25. **Person-first language:** Always seek to put the person before their disability or diagnosis. For example, instead of "a special needs child," using person-first language, you would say, "a child with special needs." Using person-first language

Communication

can help to promote respect and dignity for your child and other individuals with special needs. By emphasizing the person first, it acknowledges that individuals with special needs are unique people with strengths, interests, and challenges not defined solely by their disability.

Person-first language also helps to avoid harmful stereotypes and stigmatization that can be associated with disability labels. It recognizes that individuals with special needs are not defined by their disability and have many characteristics and attributes that make them who they are.

Using person-first language can also help to foster more positive attitudes towards individuals with special needs. It can promote greater understanding and empathy and help to break down barriers to inclusion and participation in society.

26. **Visual aids:** You can use visual aids to support communication and reinforce learning. Visual aids, including pictures, diagrams, and videos, can help your child understand and remember concepts. We know that children with special needs often struggle with following routines, leading to anxiety and frustration.

Visual schedules are a great tool to enable your child to comprehend what they need to do and in what order. Visual schedules can be created using pictures or words and placed in a prominent location where your child can easily see them. To create a visual schedule, break down your child's routine into small, manageable steps. For example, if your child's morning routine includes teeth brushing, dressing, and having breakfast, you can create a visual schedule with pictures or words for each step.

27. **Interaction:** You should encourage your child to interact with others. Encourage your child to express themselves and respond to questions. Use prompts to help your child initiate conversations. Encourage open communication and active listening between family members to create a supportive and positive atmosphere.

Help your child learn practical communication skills by modeling, practicing, and creating social opportunities. This can include role-playing, practicing conversations with family members and friends, and joining social skills groups. Take every opportunity to teach your child. For example, while walking, please encourage them to talk about the environment, read the signs, name the colors, the weather, and other visible phenomena.

28. **Chunking tasks:** Children with special needs may have difficulty understanding, so breaking down the task into smaller, more manageable steps can help them better understand and complete it. This can also help reduce anxiety and frustration. By breaking a task into smaller steps, you can help your child understand the sequence of actions required and avoid getting overwhelmed. For example, if the task is to brush their teeth, you can break it down into steps such as wetting the toothbrush, applying toothpaste, brushing each tooth, spitting out the toothpaste, and rinsing their mouth.

29. **Games:** Play games that encourage communication and language development, such as board games or card games that involve conversation. Use books with repetitive phrases or songs to reinforce language skills. Play is essential in a child's development, and incorporating play into therapy sessions can make them more engaging and effective. This can include games or activities that target specific skills or behaviors. If therapy sessions are fun and exciting, your child will be more open to participating and progressing.

In the section on technology, we explain how assistive technology, including communication apps or devices, can help children with special needs overcome barriers and communicate more effectively. You can work with your child's speech therapist or special education teacher to determine the most beneficial technology. Assistive technology can improve self-expression and social interaction.

Promoting communication skills in children with special needs requires persistence, patience, and a willingness to adapt to your child's unique needs.

By using simple language, visual aids, encouraging interaction, modeling good communication skills, using assistive technology, playing games, and sourcing speech therapy, parents can position themselves to help their children develop the skills they need to succeed.

Case Study

Communication

Tom is a 7-year-old boy with special needs. He struggles to communicate effectively with others, which often leads to frustration and misunderstandings. His parents have been working to promote his communication skills to help him express himself more clearly and improve his overall well-being.

To help Tom develop his communication skills, his parents first identified his preferred method of communication. They found that Tom responded well to visual aids, such as picture cards and sign language, rather than verbal communication alone. They then worked with a speech therapist to develop a communication plan incorporating visual aids and sign language.

Tom's parents also incorporated communication strategies into everyday activities. For example, they would use picture cards to help him identify and request items he wanted, such as a snack or a toy. They also worked on expanding his vocabulary by introducing new words and concepts in a structured, consistent manner. To reinforce these strategies, Tom's parents provided positive feedback when he successfully communicated using visual aids and sign language. They also encouraged him to use these skills in various settings, such as at home, school, and community.

Over time, Tom's communication skills improved, and he became more confident in expressing himself. As a result, his frustration levels decreased, and he could better interact with others meaningfully.

Overall, Tom's parents' use of visual aids, their incorporation of communication strategies into everyday activities, and their consistent positive reinforcement helped promote his communication skills. They improved his overall well-being and quality of life by giving him the support he needed to express himself effectively.

*If you have freedom,
free someone;
If you have power,
empower someone;
If you have light,
enlighten someone;
If you have energy,
energize someone;
If you have, do!*

—Andrea Campbell

Chapter 6

Socialization and Relationships

"Children are the world's most valuable resource and its best hope for the future"
—John F. Kennedy

Improving socialization and interpersonal relationship skills is vital for children with special needs. It helps them function more effectively and promotes inclusion in society.

My daughter participates in various extra-curricular activities, including dancing, swimming, field sports, and worship. She accompanies us to public spaces, including restaurants, leisure centers, and cultural events. In the early days, she would make loud noises which made us feel uncomfortable and apologetic, but over time we learned to manage her behavior, and she improved.

Socialization and Relationships

You also may feel that you are disrupting the public space, but you must persist so your child can have equal opportunity. Unfortunately, some members of the public do not understand or are unwilling to tolerate diversity. Still, while you should be considerate, you must not sacrifice your child's development. Be reasonable in your approach. If you and your child go to the cinema and the child is boisterous, consider leaving. There are some shows for children; in that case, staying may be acceptable.

Below are strategies you can use to build socialization and interpersonal relationship skills:

30. **Social skills building:** Encourage your child to interact with others in different social situations, such as playdates with peers, family gatherings, or community events. Encourage participation in extracurricular activities, and model appropriate social behavior. Teach your child social skills such as turn-taking, sharing, listening, and showing empathy. Practice these skills in various situations, such as at school or home. Encouraging the child to interact with peers and participate in social activities can help them to develop social skills and build relationships.

    Praise and reward your child for positive social behaviors such as sharing, taking turns, or engaging in conversation. Positive reinforcement can help your child learn and remember social skills.

31. **Role-play:** Role-play can teach your child to respond appropriately to social cues and situations. Using role-play to teach social interactions involves acting out different social scenarios with your child and providing appropriate behavior and communication feedback. Opportunities for creative problem-solving can include engaging in art activities, puzzles, or brainstorming sessions to promote critical thinking and problem-solving skills.

32. **Social scripts, social games, and social coaching:** Use social scripts to teach your child appropriate social interactions and conversation skills. Social scripts aim to teach behavioral skills, social skills, and problem-solving in a story format, relevant to the student. They can help your child develop confidence and understand social cues better, especially when their routines change.

    We have already explained the value of using games to promote communication skills. Social games involve games that require social interaction and cooperation, such as board games or role-playing games. This can help your child develop skills such as taking turns, following rules, and communicating. Social coaching

Socialization and Relationships

involves giving your child real-time feedback and guidance on appropriate social behavior. For example, "No pushing, no grabbing."

33. **Personal boundaries and safety:** Teaching your child about personal boundaries is vital for their social and emotional development. You can guide them on respecting other people's boundaries using age-appropriate language and discussing appropriate and inappropriate behavior examples.

    Teaching your child about personal safety involves educating them about potential dangers in different situations and how to stay safe. This can include teaching them how to cross the street safely, stranger danger, and what to do in an emergency. Use signs if necessary to promote understanding.

34. **Common interests:** Inspire your child to identify common interests with others, such as sports or hobbies. Participating in group activities can help your child develop friendships and social skills. Encourage them to pursue their interests and explore new activities and hobbies. Connecting with other families of special children will allow your child to socialize, build relationships with peers, and help them develop their interpersonal skills.

35. **Community involvement:** Provide opportunities for your child to get involved. Volunteering, participating in community events, or joining clubs can help your child develop socialization and interpersonal relationship skills. Seek support groups for parents of children with special needs to connect with others who understand your experiences and can provide valuable insights and advice. These groups can also offer emotional support and help reduce feelings of isolation.

36. **Extra-curricular activities:** Extracurricular activities: Encourage and inspire your child to participate in extracurricular activities such as music classes, sports, or art classes to promote socialization and build skills. Encouraging your child to try new activities and explore their interests can promote personal growth and development. It can also provide opportunities for your child to develop new friendships, build new skills and increase their self-esteem and confidence.

37. **Social skills training:** Therapists, educators, and community organizations can provide social skills training. They can provide structured programs that teach children with special needs social skills that can be practiced and applied in real-life situations. Social skills training involves teaching individuals how to interact appropriately with others in social situations. It can be

Socialization and Relationships

useful to individuals who have difficulty with communication and socialization.

In a 2016 National Library of Medicine study, four adolescents with special needs participated in a 3-week social skills intervention in both a training and a general setting. By the end of the study, all participants demonstrated substantial improvements in social skill accuracy in both settings.

Promoting socialization and interpersonal relationship skills in children with special needs requires a concerted effort from parents, educators, therapists, and the community.

By encouraging interaction, teaching social skills, using role-playing, providing positive reinforcement, finding common interests, providing opportunities for community involvement, and seeking out social skills training, parents can help their children develop the skills they need to thrive socially.

Social skills development has various benefits to children with special needs. When they learn to interact with others they improve their relationships, communication skills, and independence. Good social skills mean less challenging behavior and the potential to progress into employment opportunities.

Case Study

Emma is a 10-year-old girl with special needs. She struggles to socialize with peers and form meaningful interpersonal relationships. Her parents have been working to promote her socialization and interpersonal relationship skills to help her connect with others and improve her quality of life.

Her parents first identified her strengths and interests. They found that Emma was interested in animals and enjoyed spending time outdoors. They used these interests as a starting point for helping her connect with others.

Emma's parents then identified local community resources, such as a local nature center and a petting zoo, that offered activities and programs aligned with

Emma's interests. They signed her up for these programs and supported her to participate. Through these programs, Emma could interact with other children who shared her interests and form meaningful relationships with them. Her parents also encouraged her to invite her new friends to participate in activities with her outside of the programs. The activities included going for hikes and having playdates at home.

Emma's parents also worked with her to develop her communication and social skills. They practiced social scripts with her and worked on social cues like eye contact and turn-taking. They also provided her with positive reinforcement when she used these skills successfully.

Over time, Emma's socialization and interpersonal relationship skills improved, and she was able to form meaningful connections with peers. She became more confident and began to initiate social interactions on her own.

Emma's parents identified her strengths and interests, worked on her communication and social skills, and supported her participation in social activities in the community. Collectively these actions helped promote her socialization and interpersonal relationship skills. In addition, providing her with the support she needed to connect with others helped Emma improve her general well-being and quality of life.

Chapter 7

Behaviour Management

"Every child is gifted, they just unwrap their packages at different times"
—*Michael Carr*

Managing the behavior of children with special needs can prove challenging for parents, but there are strategies to promote positive behaviors and reduce challenging behavior.

We have had our share of challenging behavior, and though my daughter is in her mid-teens, the behavior has not stopped entirely. Different behavior management methods will work with children; there is no panacea. You have to try and learn what works for your child and accept that sometimes you may not get it right!

Behaviour Management

Some time ago, our little girl decided to turn over the basket of fruits we had on the table. She threw them on the floor without warning. After insisting that she pick them up, I decided that she should sit in a corner for a few minutes. She complied, but when I returned 7 minutes later, I found she had turned the corner into a play area. My attempt to punish her had absolutely no effect!

Below are some strategies that you may find helpful:

38. **Social modeling:** Social modeling is a technique in which you model positive behaviors and interactions for your child to imitate. Demonstrating positive behaviors and interactions can help your child learn how to interact with others positively and respectfully. Social skills training can help children learn appropriate social behaviors and interactions. This can include role-playing, modeling, and other strategies to help the child develop social skills.

39. **Behavior expectations:** You must set clear expectations for your child's behavior. This can include rules for the home, school, and community. Explain the expectations clearly and consistently, and reinforce positive behavior. Recognize your child's abilities and limitations and set goals and expectations that are reasonable and achievable. Use cards, signs, or

other media for children who do not use speech to communicate.

40. **Positive discipline:** Use discipline strategies that focus on teaching and guiding your child rather than punishing them. Communicate the rules for behavior, and provide consistent consequences for both positive and negative behavior. This can help the child understand expectations and provide a sense of structure and predictability.

41. **Positive reinforcement:** Positive reinforcement involves rewarding positive behaviors. Praise, encouragement, and rewards can motivate children with special needs to repeat positive behaviors. This can include verbal praise, hugs, stickers, treats, or other incentives. Use positive reinforcement to promote appropriate behavior.

    Positive reinforcement can be a powerful tool. Avoid using punishment and negative reinforcement, which can damage your child's self-esteem. By providing positive feedback and rewards for proper behavior, your child can develop a sense of pride and motivation to continue making good choices.

    Use behavior contracts to reinforce positive behavior and provide incentives for meeting goals. A behavior contract or agreement is made between you and your child. It outlines specific behaviors and the consequences (rewards or punishments) for meeting or failing to meet those behaviors. Many of our children cannot comprehend the idea of a written contract. In that case, do use pictures and any other media and methodology of communication that the child understands.

42. **Visual aids:** Visual aids such as charts, calendars, and pictures can help children with special needs understand and remember expectations and routines. Social stories can be a helpful tool to teach your child appropriate behavior in specific situations. Use simple, structured stories to help your child understand social situations and proper behavior. Social stories can use pictures, words, and even videos to teach your child how to react in different situations. They can help your child understand your expectations.

43. **Consistency:** Consistency is necessary for managing the behavior of children with special needs. Be consistent in your consequences, expectations, and rewards. This will help your child understand instructions and reduce confusion. Establishing a consistent routine for bedtime can help children develop healthy sleep habits. A consistent routine can also give your

child a sense of security and predictability, reducing anxiety and promoting relaxation.

44. **Calming strategies:** Children with special needs may become overwhelmed or frustrated in certain situations. Parents can teach calming techniques such as deep breathing, counting to ten, or taking breaks. These strategies can help the child regulate their emotions and behavior.

45. **Professional support:** Seek support from healthcare professionals, such as psychologists, behavior therapists, or special education teachers, if necessary. These professionals can provide strategies and tools to help manage challenging behavior.

Interdisciplinary collaboration is an approach to supporting individuals with special needs that involves professionals from multiple disciplines, such as social work, psychology, medicine, and education, working together to provide comprehensive support and services. It can benefit your child by allowing them to receive coordinated support that addresses their physical, emotional, and social needs. As a result, they can get some needs met through a combination of services, leading to better health, well-being, and overall quality of life.

In addition, collaboration among professionals from different disciplines ensures that your child benefits from the team's collective expertise, resulting in more effective and evidence-based support.

Working with professionals across disciplines is a practical approach to supporting children with special needs, providing comprehensive, coordinated, and holistic support that draws on the collective expertise of multiple professionals, leading to enhanced communication, better decision-making, and improved outcomes for individuals with special needs.

Managing the behavior of children with special needs requires patience, consistency, and a willingness to adapt to your child's unique needs. By setting clear expectations, using positive reinforcement, using visual aids, being consistent, using calming strategies, seeking out professional support, and practicing self-care, parents can help their children develop positive behaviors and manage challenging behaviors.

Although challenging behavior is one of the characteristics of special needs, there are measures that you can take to reduce the effect of this comportment.

Every child is unique, so the strategies you employ with one child may not work for another. Please consult with your child's healthcare providers and educators to develop a personalized plan for managing behavior. With the right strategies and support, parents and caregivers can help children with special needs improve their behavior, aspire higher, and reach their full potential.

Case Study

Tom is a 13-year-old boy with special needs. He often exhibits challenging behaviors, such as tantrums, aggression, and noncompliance. His parents have been struggling to manage his behavior and provide him with the support he needs to thrive.

To help manage Tom's behavior, his parents first worked closely with his healthcare team to identify the underlying causes of his challenging behaviors. They found that Tom often became frustrated and overwhelmed when he couldn't communicate his needs or understand what was happening around him. This led to outbursts and tantrums as a way of expressing his frustration.

Tom's parents then developed a behavior plan to address these underlying causes and prevent challenging behaviors from occurring. The plan included strategies such as:

- *Providing Tom with a consistent routine and structure helped him feel more secure and understand what was happening around him.*
- *Using visual aids such as picture schedules and social stories to help Tom understand what was expected of him and communicate his needs.*
- *Teaching Tom alternative communication methods, such as sign language or a communication device, to help him express his needs and feelings.*
- *Using positive reinforcement to encourage positive behaviors and discourage negative behaviors.*
- *Providing Tom with sensory supports, such as noise-canceling headphones or a sensory swing, helps him regulate his emotions and prevent sensory overload.*
- *Tom's parents also received support from a behavior specialist, who helped them*

implement the behavior plan and provided additional strategies for managing challenging behaviors.

Over time, Tom's behavior improved. The consistency of his parents in implementing the strategies outlined in the behavior plan paid off handsomely as Tom's communication improved and his frustration reduced. This positively impacted his manner, and the challenging behavior subsided.

Tom's parents' use of a behavior plan, consistent routine and structure, visual aids, alternative communication methods, positive reinforcement, sensory support, and support from a behavior specialist helped manage his behavior and improve his general well-being. Identifying and addressing the underlying causes of his challenging behavior gave him the support he needed to thrive.

We can mother and we can mentor, but it's when we model that we make the greatest impact.

—Andrea Campbell

Chapter 8

Emotional and Mental Health

"Start where you are. Use what you have. Do what you can"
—*Arthur Ashe*

Managing children's emotional and mental health is an essential aspect of parenting. It is a process that requires patience, understanding, and love.

We discovered very early that our daughter did not tolerate interpersonal conflict well. Her dad and I were arguing one day, and she started to cry. Since then, we have endeavored to avoid arguing in her presence. This has had a positive effect on our family, as we have avoided arguing since then.

Even an animated conversation is upsetting to our little girl. When she was eight, we had a vibrant discussion

Emotional and Mental Health

that appeared to her as if we were arguing. She shouted to us, "Stop it!" That was amazing. We assured her that we were talking, and then we toned it down. Even if your child is non-verbal, you must never assume that your words do not hurt them. Remember, the fact that they are not speaking doesn't mean they are not understanding or that they have nothing to say!

Protecting your child's emotional and mental health helps them thrive and aspire to higher goals. Here are some strategies:

46. **Nurturing and supportive environment:** Creating a supportive and nurturing environment at home can help promote emotional and mental well-being for your child. This can include a stable routine, a calm and positive atmosphere, and plenty of love and affection. For example, establish predictable routines and schedules for daily activities such as mealtimes, bedtime, and homework. In addition, creating a calm-down space at home where your child can relax and manage stress can be helpful. This can involve creating a quiet, comfortable area where they can engage in calming activities such as reading or listening to music.

47. **Safe and accessible physical environment:** Make sure your home is safe and accessible for your child. For example: Do you need adaptations to make your home more comfortable or an area

where your child can relax and unwind when necessary? Is your home environment peaceful and calm, and do you need to add structures that minimize noise and distractions? Many children with special needs struggle with sensory overload. Creating a sensory-friendly environment at home and in public spaces can help reduce stress and promote comfort.

48. **Expression of emotions:** Children with special needs may have difficulty expressing their emotions. Do encourage your child to express their emotions by providing a supportive, safe environment for them to do so. This can include using social stories, visual aids, or role-playing to help them understand and express their emotions.

49. **Physical activity:** Regular physical activity improves mental health and reduces stress. Support your child to participate in physical activity appropriate for their abilities and interests. This could include walking, swimming, or yoga. Allowing movement breaks can also help your child regulate their energy levels and improve focus. This can consist of simple activities such as stretching or walking.

50. **Coping strategies:** Children with special needs may struggle with stress or anxiety. Teach your child coping strategies such as mindfulness, deep breathing, or guided imagery. These strategies

Emotional and Mental Health

can help them regulate their emotions and reduce stress. Practicing mindfulness techniques such as journaling, yoga, or meditation can promote relaxation and reduce stress for you and your child. You can also find mindfulness apps or videos specifically designed for children.

51. **External support:** If your child is experiencing significant emotional or mental health issues, seeking support from a mental health professional may be helpful. An appropriate health professional can provide support and guidance to help your child manage their emotions and mental health.

    You should elicit support from family and friends to meet your child's needs and reduce stress on yourself. Finally, pay attention to the ever-expanding online community of parents who are an excellent resource for parents of children with special needs.

52. **Self-care:** Managing the behavior of and caring for a special child can take a toll. You need to practice self-care and take time for yourself. Practice stress-management techniques to help you cope with the challenges of parenting a special child. This can include exercise, meditation, deep breathing, taking breaks, or talking with a supportive friend or therapist.

Endeavor to build a robust support system by connecting with family, friends, and professionals who can provide emotional and practical support. It is also helpful to foster positive relationships with teachers and caregivers to ensure open communication and collaboration regarding your child's care and education. Establish a self-care routine that allows you to maintain your physical and mental health. This may include activities such as meditation, exercise, or spending time with friends and family.

53. **Respite care:** Respite care is a form of short-term relief for caregivers. Respite care services are typically provided by trained professionals who can offer additional support and guidance to families of individuals with special needs. It involves providing temporary care and support for individuals with special needs so that their family members or caregivers can have a break from their caregiving responsibilities.

Respite care can provide a temporary break from caregiving responsibilities, giving family members time to recharge and reduce stress. Moreover, respite care can help strengthen family relationships by reducing the strain from caregiving responsibilities and allowing family members to spend quality time without the demands of caregiving.

54. **Self-education:** Educating yourself about your child's special needs and co-occurring mental health conditions can help you better understand and support your child. Work with your child's healthcare providers to learn the best practices for managing their emotional and mental health.

Managing the emotional and mental health of children with special needs requires a holistic approach that includes creating a supportive environment, encouraging the expression of emotions, promoting physical activity, teaching coping strategies, seeking professsional support, practicing self-care, and educating yourself about your child's needs.

Using these strategies, parents can help their children thrive emotionally and mentally.

Case Study

Emily is a 9-year-old girl with special needs. She often struggles with anxiety, making her unable to participate in social activities and feel confident. However, Emily's parents' support has significantly improved her emotional and mental health.

Emily's parents worked closely with her healthcare team to develop an individualized plan to promote her emotional and mental health. They identified strategies to help Emily manage her anxiety and feel more confident. One of the key strategies they used was to provide Emily with a safe and supportive environment at home. They made sure she had a quiet and comfortable space where she could relax and feel at ease, and they provided her with a consistent routine and structure to help her feel more secure.

Emily's parents also worked with her to develop coping strategies for managing her anxiety. For example, they taught her deep breathing exercises and mindfulness techniques, which helped her calm her mind and reduce her anxiety. They also worked with her to identify triggers for her anxiety and develop strategies for managing them.

In addition to these strategies, Emily's parents emphasized the importance of social support. They encouraged her to participate in activities with her peers and provided opportunities to socialize in a safe and supportive environment. They also worked with her to develop social skills and confidence, which helped her feel more comfortable in social situations.

Through the implementation of these strategies, Emily was able to make significant improvements in her emotional and mental health. She became more confident in herself and her abilities and learned strategies for managing her anxiety and stress. In addition, her parents found that their support and encouragement helped improve her overall well-being and quality of life.

In summary, Emily's parents' use of a safe and supportive environment, coping strategies, and social support helped improve her emotional and mental health. In addition, by working closely with her healthcare team and focusing on strategies that worked for Emily, her parents were able to help her achieve her full emotional and mental potential.

Chapter 9

Physical Health and Mobility

"Movement is the song of the body."
—*Vanda Scaravelli*

Managing the physical health and mobility of children with special needs is important for several reasons. First, our children have poorer health and more significant health needs than the general population and are at greater risk for weight and lifestyle-related problems.

According to Special Education expert John Simpson, individuals with special needs are more likely than others to live an inactive lifestyle and are less likely to be physically fit. Individuals with special needs are more likely to be overweight (or in some cases underweight) and are at higher risk for illnesses and diseases related to weight-related conditions, he said.

We are a working family but find time to take our child to extra-curricular activities. She participates in swimming, dancing, music classes, and field sports. She has been away to camp, and on one occasion, she returned with the "Best Dancer" award. The following year she got the "Best Mountaineer" award.

Our children often cannot compete with neurotypical kids, but don't be discouraged, for they are running their own race at their pace. Here are some strategies that parents can use to support their child's physical health and mobility:

55. **Regular physical activity:** This is essential for overall health and well-being and can help children with special needs maintain a healthy weight, strengthen muscles, and improve cardiovascular health. Please encourage your child to engage in physical activity appropriate for their abilities and interests, such as walking, swimming, or adaptive sports, to help them develop their coordination, strength, and social skills.

56. **Healthy diet:** A healthy diet is needed for maintaining physical health. Provide a balanced and nutritious diet, including whole grains, vegetables, lean proteins, fruits, and healthy fats. Consult a dietitian or healthcare professional to guide your child's nutritional needs.

57. **Medical check-ups:** Regular medical check-ups can help ensure your child's health is adequately monitored. Schedule regular appointments with a pediatrician or other healthcare professional specializing in children with special needs.

58. **Management of co-occurring medical conditions:** Children with special needs may be more prone to certain medical conditions, such as seizures, sleep disorders, or gastrointestinal issues. Work with your child's healthcare provider to manage co-occurring medical

Physical Health and Mobility

conditions and ensure that your child receives appropriate treatment.

59. **Assistive devices and adaptations:** Assistive devices and adaptations can help children with special needs maintain mobility and independence. This may include mobility aids such as wheelchairs, walkers, or canes and modifications to the home environment to promote accessibility and safety.

60. **Good hygiene:** Hygiene is essential for maintaining physical health and preventing the spread of illness. Encourage your child to practice good hygiene habits such as hand washing, tooth brushing, and bathing. Remember to use a deodorant with your child. It may be helpful if you consult your healthcare provider to get advice on which deodorant to use. Some children cannot tolerate aluminum, commonly used in deodorants.

61. **Advocacy:** Advocate for your child's physical health and mobility needs. This may include working with your child's school or other community organizations to ensure that they have access to appropriate accommodations and support. Build a team of professionals, including therapists and doctors, to support your child's development and well-being. Work with your

child's team to create an individualized plan addressing their needs and goals.

Managing the physical health and mobility of children with special needs requires a holistic approach that includes encouraging physical activity, providing a healthy diet, scheduling regular medical check-ups, managing co-occurring medical conditions, providing assistive devices and adaptations, practicing good hygiene, and advocating for your child. By implementing these strategies, parents can help their children maintain good physical health and mobility.

You must truly understand your child to manage your special child's physical health and mobility effectively. Work with healthcare providers and educators to develop a personalized plan for managing your child's physical health and mobility. With the appropriate

Physical Health and Mobility

strategies and support, you can you're your child maintain good physical health and mobility, improving their general quality of life.

Case Study

Max is a 12-year-old boy with special needs. He has low muscle tone and difficulty with balance and coordination, making physical activity challenging. However, with the support of his parents and the healthcare team, Max has significantly improved his physical health and mobility.

Max's parents worked closely with his healthcare team to develop an individualized plan to improve his physical health and mobility. They identified specific exercises and activities that would help Max build strength, balance, and coordination, and they regularly worked with him on these activities.

One of the key strategies they used was to make physical activity fun and engaging for Max. For example, they introduced him to adapted sports tailored to his abilities, such as wheelchair basketball and swimming. Max enjoyed these activities and looked forward to participating, which helped him stay motivated and engaged.

Max's parents also ensured he had access to the equipment and resources necessary to be physically active. For example, they worked with his healthcare team to obtain a specialized wheelchair that was comfortable and supportive, which allowed him to participate in sports and other physical activities. They also ensured he had appropriate footwear, clothing, and other assistive devices to move around safely and comfortably.

Finally, Max's parents emphasized the importance of healthy habits, such as good nutrition and getting enough rest. They worked with him to develop healthy eating habits and ensured he got enough sleep each night to help his body recover and recharge. Through the use of these strategies, Max was able to improve his physical health and mobility. As a result, he gained strength and coordination and became more confident in moving around and participating in physical activities. In addition, Max's parents found that these activities and healthy habits helped improve his overall well-being and quality of life.

Max's parents used an individualized plan, engaged in physical activity, accessed appropriate equipment and resources, and practiced healthy habits to promote his physical health and mobility. In addition, by working closely with his healthcare team and emphasizing fun and engagement, they were able to help Max improve his physical prowess.

Motivation gets you going, passion keeps you growing, but it's persistence that gets you there.

—Andrea Campbell

Chapter 10

Technology and Adaptations

*"It's not a faith in technology.
It's faith in people"*
—*Steve Jobs*

Technology and adaptations are helpful tools for supporting the development and independence of children with special needs. Henrietta Fore, Executive Director of UNICEF, recently stated, "Assistive technology like wheelchairs, prosthetics, hearing aids, and glasses give people with disabilities a chance to overcome barriers and demonstrate what they can do rather than what they cannot." UNICEF has a long track record of research and evidence on children with disabilities.

Technology and Adaptations

All the children in our neighborhood ride bikes. They start with tricycles and quickly graduate to bicycles. My little girl couldn't balance a bike, so she has a specially-made and adapted trike. It was pricier than the others, but it allowed her equal opportunity and inclusion. As parents of special children, we should be prepared to go the extra mile for our children to improve their life chances.

Here are some ways that parents can use technology and adaptations to support their children:

62. **Assistive technology:** This refers to devices and software that can help individuals with disabilities perform tasks that might otherwise be challenging. Examples of assistive technology include speech-to-text software, communication apps, and adapted computer peripherals such as keyboards and mice. These technologies can help your child communicate, learn, and easily access information.

    Appropriate assistive technology directly impacts children's well-being by supporting their functionality and inclusion into society, increase-ing opportunities for education, employment, and social engagement.

63. **Visual supports:** Visual supports such as pictures, icons, and schedules can be helpful for children with special needs who struggle with

language or communication. You can use visual supports to help your child understand routines and expectations, communicate their needs and preferences, and learn new skills.

64. **Adapted materials:** Adapting materials such as books, worksheets, and games can help make learning more accessible. Examples of adaptations might include simplifying language, using visual supports, or modifying tasks to be more achievable for the child.

65. **Augmentative and alternative communication (AAC):** AAC refers to tools and techniques that support communication for individuals with difficulty speaking or writing. Examples of AAC include picture-based communication boards, sign language, and voice output devices. AAC can benefit your child if they struggle with expressive language.

66. **Virtual resources and support:** With the rise of teletherapy and virtual resources, you can access a range of support services for your child without leaving home. This might include virtual therapy sessions, online support groups, or web-based training resources.

When using technology and adaptations to support your child, working with a team of professionals, including educators, therapists, and assistive

Technology and Adaptations

technology specialists, is helpful. These professionals can guide the selection and implementation of appropriate technologies and adaptations and provide ongoing support for the child and their family.

By collaborating with professionals involved in the care and teaching of your child, you can develop a personalized plan for engaging with technology and relevant adaptations to support your child. The aim is to help your child access the appropriate support to enable them to live a fulfilling life.

Case Study

Sarah is a 9-year-old girl with Down syndrome. She struggles with reading and writing, making it challenging to keep up with her peers in school. However, with the help of technology and adapta-

tions, Sarah has improved her academic skills and gained greater independence.

Sarah's parents worked closely with her teachers and educational specialists to identify the specific areas where Sarah needed support. They determined that Sarah would benefit from technology and other adaptations to help her access and understand the curriculum.

One of the adaptations that Sarah's family introduced was a tablet device with specialized educational software. This software provided Sarah with interactive reading and writing activities tailored to her ability level. The tablet also had a text-to-speech function that allowed Sarah to listen to books and other materials, improving her comprehension and vocabulary.

Another adaptation that Sarah's family introduced was a set of visual aids. These included picture schedules, checklists, and visual prompts that helped Sarah stay organized and focused. For example, Sarah's family created a morning routine checklist, which included brushing her teeth and getting dressed. The visual prompts helped Sarah complete these tasks independently without constant reminders from her parents.

Through the use of technology and adaptations, Sarah was able to gain greater independence and improve *her academic skills. As a result, she completed assignments more efficiently and effectively and felt more confident in her abilities. In addition, Sarah's family found that these adaptations helped reduce her frustration and anxiety, which improved her overall well-being.*

Sarah's family's use of technology and adaptations provided her with the tools and support she needed to succeed academically and develop independence. Also, by working closely with her teachers and educational specialists, the parents identified the specific areas where Sarah needed support and were able to address the issue.

Chapter 11

Family Support

"Families are the compass that guide us. They are the inspiration to reach great heights, and our comfort when we occasionally falter"
—Brad Henry

Family and support are crucial in raising a child with special needs. Family is a critical source of support for children with disabilities. They can help with the added demands on time, emotional, and financial resources of raising a child with special needs. Through this emotional support, access to resources, advocacy, education, skill-building, and building a sense of belonging, family members and caregivers can help children with special needs.

When my daughter was born, I was happy but uncertain about the future. We were lucky to have

Family Support

family support in those early years. My sisters-in-law often kept the baby and gave me time to heal emotionally and physically. The help I received in the first year allowed me to settle quite quickly into my role as the mom of a special child.

Family support can be helpful in a range of ways:

67. **Emotional support:** Raising a child with special needs can be challenging and emotionally taxing. A robust support system consisting of family, friends, and professionals can help parents and caregivers manage stress and emotional strain.

68. **Breaks:** As a parent, taking care of yourself is particularly important to provide the best care for your child. This may include seeking respite care from family, friends, or professionals, taking breaks when needed, and focusing on self-care activities such as exercise or relaxation. Always seek support when needed, provided that support is safe and available. Being absent from your child's presence does not equate to you being a bad parent; it just gives you time to recharge.

You can practice relaxation techniques such as deep breathing, meditation, progressive muscle relaxation, or guided imagery as a family to promote peace and reduce stress for everyone. This is particularly helpful when there is heightened anxiety or when dealing with challenging situations.

69. **Access to resources:** Families of children with special needs often require various resources and support services to help their child thrive. These include access to healthcare, therapy, education, and assistive technology. Support from family and others can help ensure the child can access the resources they need to thrive.

70. **Advocacy support:** Family members and other caregivers can advocate for your child, ensuring their needs are met and treated with respect and dignity. Advocacy might include working with schools and other organizations to ensure the child receives appropriate accommodations and support or advocating for policies and funding.

71. **Education and skill-building:** Family members and caregivers can play a key role in supporting your child's learning and independence building. This might include working on communication and socialization skills, providing opportunities for play and recreation, or teaching daily living skills such as cooking and hygiene.

72. **Sense of belonging:** Children with special needs may struggle with socialization and building meaningful relationships. Family members and caregivers can help create a sense

Family Support

of belonging by fostering positive relationships with the child. They can also support your child to participate in activities and events, connecting them with social opportunities in the community.

73. **Emotional support:** Having special needs can be challenging, so you must provide emotional support to your child. This might include listening to the child's concerns, offering encouragement, and showing love and affection. Emotional support helps children feel loved, valued and included. And while you recognize this as your role, you should know that it is ok if they also get that support from other people.

74. **Educational support:** Families can be essential in supporting their child's education. This might involve working with teachers and other professionals to develop an individualized education plan (IEP) that addresses the child's unique needs and goals or providing additional support and resources at home to help the child learn.

75. **Independence support:** While children with special needs may require additional support, it is important to promote independence and self-reliance. This might involve teaching daily living skills such as cooking and hygiene or providing opportunities for the child to engage in age-appropriate activities.

76. **Identification of resources:** Many resources are available to support families of children with special needs, such as support groups, advocacy organizations, and educational resources. Families can look for these resources to help them navigate the various challenges of raising a child with special needs.

Supporting a child with special needs requires a multi-faceted approach that involves emotional support, advocacy, education, and independence-building. Developing a support system of family, friends, and professionals can provide you and your child with emotional support, resources, and guidance. In addition, it can help you feel less isolated and more connected to your community.

Consider working together with your family to help your child thrive.

Case Study

John is a 12-year-old boy with special needs. He struggles with social interactions and communication, making forming friendships and participating in group activities difficult. However, with family support, John was able to thrive and overcome some of the challenges he faced.

John's parents have been a key source of support for him. They have worked closely with his teachers and therapists to develop an individualized education plan that meets his needs. John's parents also actively participate in his therapy sessions, providing encouragement and support as he learns new skills.

In addition to working with professionals, John's family has created a supportive environment at home. They have established clear routines and expectations.

which helps John feel more secure and comfortable in his daily life. John's family also tries to provide him with opportunities for socialization and engagement, such as taking him to community events or inviting his classmates over for playdates.

One example of how family support has helped John is his sports participation. While John initially struggled to find a sport he enjoyed and could participate in, his family encouraged him to try various activities. Eventually, they discovered that John had a natural talent for swimming, and they began to support him in pursuing this interest. As a result, John's family regularly attends his swim meets and provides him with positive feedback and encouragement. Through this support, John has improved his physical health and developed greater self-confidence and social skills.

John's family has played a crucial role in his development and success. By working closely with professionals, creating a supportive environment at home, and providing opportunities for engagement and growth, John's family has helped him overcome some of the challenges he faces due to his special needs. As a result, John can lead a more fulfilling and rewarding life.

Love says yes and love says no; love holds on and love lets go. Love is being and love is doing; love is really understanding.

—Andrea Campbell

Chapter 12

Self-esteem and Personal Growth

"Doing the best at this moment puts you in the best place for the next moment"
—*Oprah Winfrey*

Self-esteem makes us feel content with ourselves, like ourselves, and feel a sense of purpose. It makes us feel worthwhile, valuable and feel that we matter. Therefore, building self-esteem in a child with special needs can help them feel good about themselves and their abilities.

I take every opportunity to praise my child for her accomplishments. When she brings home her schoolwork, I tell her I am proud of her. I use applause and hugs to show her my appreciation for her efforts. When we do academic work at home, I shower her with tangible and non-tangible rewards. She is encouraged

Self-esteem and Personal Growth

to do her best, whatever the outcome. One year she was one of eight children from her school to receive a national award for outstanding work. We had a party to celebrate her achievement!

Parents can help build self-esteem and encourage personal growth in their disabled children in the following ways:

77. **Celebrations**: Praising and celebrating their child's accomplishments, no matter how small, can boost their self-esteem and motivate them to continue trying new things.

    Focus on your child's strengths and talents and encourage and inspire them to pursue their interests and passions. When your child achieves a goal or makes progress, celebrate their success. Recognize and acknowledge their efforts, and provide positive reinforcement to promote further growth. For example, give them a high five, a hug, or a special treat.

    Celebrating their achievements shows your child that you are proud of them and that their efforts are valued. Celebrating accomplishments, no matter how small, can help build a child's self-esteem and motivate them to continue learning. Parents should provide positive feedback and praise for their child's efforts, progress, and achievements.

78. **Encouragement of independence**: Encouraging children to try new things independently, with support when necessary, can build confidence and foster a sense of freedom. In this regard, it is helpful to employ a strength-based approach that focuses on identifying and building on an individual's strengths, abilities, and resources rather than focusing solely on their deficits or limitations. This strength-based approach can help your child recognize and celebrate their strengths, increasing self-esteem, confidence, and greater motivation to engage in activities and pursue goals. In addition, it helps children identify their passions and interests, leading to a greater sense of purpose and fulfillment.

79. **Goal setting**: Setting achievable, personalized goals for your child, recognizing their unique strengths, and tracking their progress can provide a feeling of accomplishment and encourage personal growth. Start with single-step goals such as "remove your shoes." In time you can add "put them away."

80. **Socialization opportunities**: Socialization with peers and community members can help children develop social skills and build positive relationships, enhancing their self-esteem. A strength-based approach has been shown to

improve social skills, increase independence, and boost engagement in meaningful activities.

81. **Opportunities for creative expression**: Encourage your child to express themselves creatively through song, poetry, art, music, and other forms of self-expression. This can help them develop their emotional and cognitive abilities while providing a source of enjoyment and relaxation.

82. **Strengths and interests**: Focusing on your child's strengths and abilities, rather than their limitations, can help them develop a positive self-image and build self-esteem. Identifying your child's strengths and providing opportunities to excel in areas that come naturally to them is essential. This will help build confidence and self-esteem, which will be important in overcoming challenges. Also, you can help your child develop their talents and passions by focusing on their strengths and interests. This approach can boost their confidence and motivation, leading to tremendous success in academic and personal pursuits.

83. **Encouragement of creativity**: When you provide for your child opportunities for creative expressions, such as art, music, and drama, you promote their personal growth and help them develop new skills and interests.

84. **Positive language**: When talking to your child, use positive language to promote self-esteem and a positive self-image. Focus on their strengths and accomplishments and avoid using negative language or criticism. Instead, provide positive feedback and constructive criticism to help your child build self-awareness and encourage personal growth. Use positive and empowering language to communicate with your child. Concentrate firmly on what your child can do rather than can't. For instance, instead of saying, "You can't do that," say, "Let's try it together."

85. **Self-esteem modeling**: Model positive self-esteem by speaking positively about yourself and others. Do not engage in any mean language in your child's presence. Be a good role model and help your child develop a healthy self-image.

When you help your child build self-esteem, you empower them to enjoy many benefits for their overall well-being and success. A child with high self-esteem is resilient—an essential skill they will need to counter bullies, for example. The child will be more motivated and confident to try new tasks. Self-esteem generates happiness, joy, and improved well-being. All this can lead to better academic prowess.

Building self-esteem and encouraging personal growth in your child requires a supportive and positive

Self-esteem and Personal Growth

environment, opportunities for growth and socialization, and a focus on their strengths and abilities. Empower your child to reach their full potential and lead a fulfilling life by providing these opportunities.

Case Study

Sophie is a 7-year-old girl with special needs. She struggles with learning new skills and often feels frustrated when she cannot do things independently. Sophie's mother, Maria, has been working with her to build her self-esteem and encourage personal growth.

One way that Maria has built Sophie's self-esteem is by focusing on her strengths and accomplishments. Even small achievements, such as completing a puzzle or tying her shoes, are celebrated and praised. By highlighting Sophie's strengths and progress, Maria has helped her develop a sense of pride in her abilities and feel more confident.

Another way that Maria has built Sophie's self-esteem is by encouraging her to try new things and take risks. While Sophie can be hesitant to try new activities, Maria has found that encouraging her to explore new interests can help build her self-confidence. For example, Maria enrolled Sophie in a dance class, even though Sophie was initially nervous and unsure about it. However, as Sophie started to learn new dance moves and connect with other children in the class, her self-esteem began to grow.

Maria has also found that providing Sophie with independence opportunities helped build her self-esteem. While Sophie may struggle with specific tasks, such as tying her shoes or getting dressed, Maria encourages her to do as much as she can independently. By allowing Sophie to take ownership of her tasks and accomplishments, Maria has helped her develop a sense of pride and independence.

Maria's efforts to build Sophie's self-esteem have positively impacted her personal growth and development. By focusing on Sophie's strengths, encouraging her to try new things, and providing opportunities for independence, Maria has helped Sophie feel more confident and capable. As a result, Sophie has overcome some of the challenges she faces due to her special needs and now leads a more fulfilling life.

Chapter 13

Community Involvement and Resources

"History will judge us by the difference we make in the everyday lives of children"
—Nelson Mandela

Community involvement and resources can be vital in empowering kids with special needs and their families. Communities can help children with special needs aspire higher by providing access to specialized services.

As a family, we are involved in planning events for the community. We sit on boards, attend meetings and focus groups and ensure that the voice of disabled people are heard. Without families like ours in these strategic spaces, special needs planning is void of

Community Involvement and Resources

depth, and our children and young people will fall victim to inertia.

I recently participated in a meeting to design a play area in the community. When the committee presented the draft, there was no consideration for people with wheelchairs, and the equipment was not friendly to disabled people. Had I not been there, the planning would have gone ahead, and our young people would have been excluded.

Community involvement helps to break down barriers and reduce the stigma surrounding special needs. When children with special needs are included and valued in their communities, it can help promote a more inclusive and accepting society. When we get it right, we get to live in a healthy and wholesome environment.

Community involvement and resources can come in many forms. Here are some examples:

86. **Advocate for inclusion**: You should advocate for policies that support inclusive education and access to services in your community. This could also involve collaborating with schools, healthcare providers, and other community organizations to ensure your child and his peers have the necessary support and resources. It could also extend to your child's inclusion in school activities and community events. This helps your child develop social skills, make friends, and feel valued as a community member, which will be

crucial for their long-term success and well-being.

87. **Access to specialized services**: Many communities have specialized services for children with special needs. These services include therapy, educational programs, and recreational activities. These services can give your child the support they need to develop new skills.

88. **Peer support**: Community involvement can allow children to interact with peers with similar experiences and challenges. This can help them develop social skills, build friendships, and feel a sense of belonging. Parents can also benefit from peer support. Seek and find support groups for parents of children with special needs. Parents who understand your journey can be great help and advice. Find support groups in your locale or online. Such groups provide a safe space to share your experiences and connect with others facing similar challenges.

89. **Education and awareness**: Community involvement can help raise awareness and educate others about special needs. You could volunteer to design fliers and plan events that are inclusive for all. This can lead to greater acceptance, understanding, and support for kids with special needs and their families.

90. **Resources for families**: Communities often have resources available to support families- support groups, respite care, and financial assistance. These resources can help families navigate the complexities of raising a special child and provide additional support when needed. Other families of children with special needs can be valuable sources of support. Join a local parents' group or online community to access opportunities for sharing experiences, advice, and resources.

91. **Employment and work experience**: As your child grows into adulthood, community involvement can provide access to employment, work experience opportunities, and job training programs. This can help them develop skills, gain independence, and contribute to their communities. In addition, employment can give your child a renewed sense of purpose and help them feel valued and valuable.

92. **Volunteering opportunities**: Volunteering can be an excellent way for your child to gain new skills, make social connections, and give back to their community. In addition to enhancing and building technical skills, they will improve their social skills as they interact with other volunteers and the people they serve. As they establish new social connections, they will feel more included,

strengthening their self-esteem and confidence and improving their general well-being. Volunteering will result in mental stimulation, which can improve physical and psychological health. Volunteering is also an excellent way for your child to secure paid employment.

Community involvement and resources can give your child and your family a sense of belonging, support, and opportunity.

By working together, communities can help create a more inclusive and supportive environment for all children, including those with special needs.

Case Study

Marcie is a 10-year-old girl with special needs. She struggles with communication and socialization and often feels isolated and misunderstood. Marcie's parents have been working with her school and healthcare providers to provide her with the support she needs, but they have also found that community involvement has been critical in helping Marcie thrive.

One way that community involvement has helped Marcie is through her participation in a local dance class. Marcie loves to dance but has struggled to find opportunities to participate in traditional dance classes due to her disability. However, a local dance studio offers an adaptive dance class specifically for children with disabilities, which has been a perfect fit for Marcie.

In the adaptive dance class, Marcie can participate in a supportive environment tailored to her needs. The dance instructor has experience working with children with disabilities and can provide modifications and accommodations to help Marcie succeed. Marcie has also been able to make friends with other children in the class, which has helped her develop social skills and build self-confidence.

In addition to the dance class, Marcie's parents have also found support through a local parent support group for families of children with special needs. The support group allows families to share their experiences and connect with others who understand the unique challenges of raising a child with special needs. Through the support group, Marcie's parents have been able to access resources and advice from other parents, which has been invaluable in helping them navigate the sometimes overwhelming world of special needs parenting.

Community involvement has played a critical role in helping Marcie thrive. Through the adaptive dance class, Marcie has been able to develop social skills, build self-confidence, and find a sense of belonging. Her parents have also found support and resources through the community, which has helped them better understand and support Marcie's needs. Through community involvement, Marcie has overcome the barriers she faces due to her special needs and now leads a more fulfilling life.

*If you can't do it alone,
do it together;
and if you can't go
together, go it alone.*

—Andrea Campbell

Chapter 14

Supplementary Therapies

"Do the best you can until you know better. Then when you know better, do better"

—*Maya Angelou*

Engagement in supplementary therapies can improve your child's physical, emotional, and social well-being, leading to a better quality of life. These therapies can help your child develop new skills and abilities, such as enhanced communication or motor skills, increasing their independence and allowing them to participate more fully in daily activities. For example, better movement and communication will improve their social skills, help them find meaningful friendships, and develop a sense of belonging. In addition, specific therapies can help your child regulate their emotions and manage symptoms of anxiety, depression, and other mental health concerns.

When accessing supplementary therapies, working with a qualified therapist or practitioner is essential to determine which therapies may be most beneficial for your child. When my daughter was younger, we consulted a therapist to ascertain whether she could participate in horseback riding. She gave us some guidelines, and we booked the activity. My daughter was happy to pet the horse but refused to ride. Sometimes with the best of intentions, we have to amend and adapt our aspirations. There are horses for courses, and this just wasn't one for her.

It is important to remember that therapy should be used with other treatments and support and that progress may take time and patience. Our final set of tips covers some supplementary therapies that may be beneficial for your child:

93. **Music therapy**: Music therapy involves using music to address physical, emotional, cognitive, and social needs. It can improve your child's communication, motor skills, and overall well-being.

    Music therapy helps individuals with special needs improve their communication skills by encouraging verbal and nonverbal expression through music. This can lead to improved social interaction and self-expression. This type of therapy can improve cognitive function in individuals by stimulating the areas of the brain that deal with memory and attention, which can lead to enhanced learning, problem-solving, and decision-making. It helps regulate emotions by providing a safe and non-threatening way for your child to express their feelings. Finally, it provides sensory stimulation for individuals by engaging multiple senses, such as hearing, touch, and movement.

94. **Art therapy**: Art therapy involves using art as a means of expression, communication, and emotional healing. It can improve your child's social skills, self-esteem, and emotional regulation.

    Art therapy can help individuals with cognitive disabilities improve their emotional regulation by providing a safe and supportive environment to explore and express their emotions through art-making. It can increase their self-awareness by providing a creative outlet for self-expression and exploring their thoughts and feelings. It can improve their communication skills by providing a non-verbal means of expression and promoting using visual aids to communicate.

    Art therapy can increase your child's self-esteem by creating something unique and celebrating their artistic achievements. Finally, art therapy can help to improve your child's cognitive skills, such as attention and memory, through art-making exercises that require sustained attention and concentration.

95. **Animal-assisted therapy**: Animal-assisted therapy involves working with animals to achieve therapeutic goals. It incorporates animals, such as dogs or horses, into therapy sessions and can benefit those with special needs by improving social skills, communication, and well-being. In addition, it can enable your child to improve their social skills by providing opportunities for interaction with animals and people in a structured and supportive environment.

The presence of animals during therapy sessions can be motivating, and children are often more engaged and willing to participate in therapy activities when animals are involved. In addition, animals can provide emotional support through companionship, unconditional love, and non-judgmental acceptance. This can particularly benefit those struggling with social interaction and emotional regulation.

Touching and petting the animals can provide tactile input and help your child regulate their sensory systems. This kind of therapy can involve activities such as horseback riding or walking a dog, which can provide physical activity and exercise. In addition, interacting with animals has been shown to reduce anxiety and stress.

96. **Dance/movement therapy:** This kind of therapy involves using movement as a medium of expression and communication. It can be helpful for people with special needs as it can improve social skills, motor skills, mobility, physical functioning, and overall well-being. It also provides a great medium for socialization and interaction with others. This can lead to increased social skills and a sense of belonging. However, engaging with a qualified music therapist is necessary to determine if dance therapy is appropriate and safe for your child's unique needs and goals.

97. **Sensory integration therapy**: Sensory integration therapy involves using play and sensory experiences to help individuals process and integrate sensory information from their environment and organize their sensory systems. It can benefit people who have difficulty processing sensory information and improve their ability to participate in daily activities. For example, your child may be overly sensitive to sensory inputs like loud noises or bright lights. This can cause them to feel overwhelmed or anxious, resulting in challenging behavior or a shutdown response.

Sensory integration therapy can help by providing them with sensory experiences in a structured and controlled environment. The therapy aims to improve their ability to regulate and organize sensory input, enhancing their ability to participate in daily activities and reduce negative behaviors.

During sensory integration therapy, an occupational therapist may use activities such as swinging, spinning, or playing with sensory toys to help your child learn how to process and respond to sensory input in a more adaptive way. The therapist may also work on developing other skills, such as balance and coordination, which can benefit your child. Sensory integration therapy can be a useful tool to improve daily functioning and quality of life.

98. **Cognitive behavioral therapy**: The aim of Cognitive behavioral therapy (CBT) is to change negative thoughts, beliefs, and behaviors to improve mental health and well-being. This involves working with individuals to identify and modify negative thought patterns and behaviors. It can help people who struggle with anxiety, depression, or other mental health concerns.

CBT can be useful for people with special needs because it can help them improve their emotional regulation by teaching them how to identify and challenge negative beliefs and thoughts that contribute to emotional distress. It can also improve problem-solving skills by teaching individuals how to chunk down problems into smaller parts and develop practical solutions.

CBT helps build social skills by teaching people to communicate effectively and assertively and manage social anxiety and interpersonal conflict. It can help your child develop greater self-awareness by identifying their strengths and weaknesses and understanding how their thoughts and behaviors impact their emotions and well-being. This can lead to a reduction in problem behavior.

99. **Play therapy**: Play therapy involves using play as a means of expression and communication to help individuals. It can be helpful for your child as it can improve social skills, emotional regulation, and overall well-being. This form of therapy allows self-expression and provides opportunities to work through emotional and behavioral challenges. It enhances communication skills by providing a nonverbal expression that is less intimidating than traditional talk therapy.

Through play, individuals can communicate their thoughts, feelings, and experiences and improve their emotional regulation by exploring and expressing complex emotions in a safe and supportive environment. Play therapy can help individuals with cognitive disabilities increase their social skills by providing opportunities for interaction, collaboration, learning turn-taking, sharing, and undertaking problem-solving exercises. It can help individuals improve their cognitive skills, including attention, memory, and problem-solving, through activities designed to stimulate these areas. Play therapy can help those with mental disabilities increase their self-esteem by providing opportunities for success and mastery in a fun and engaging way.

100. **Recreational therapy**: Recreational therapy involves leisure activities to improve physical, emotional, and social well-being. It can be beneficial for your child as it provides opportunities for socialization, physical activity, and skill development.

    Recreational therapy, also known as therapeutic recreation, can help improve your child's physical health by engaging in activities that promote physical fitness and wellness, such as swimming, hiking, or yoga. This type of therapy can improve social skills by providing opportunities for interaction and building social connections through shared activities.

Recreational therapy can increase independence by developing decision-making, problem-solving, and self-advocacy skills through cooking or gardening. It can also help improve cognitive skills, such as attention, memory, and problem-solving, through activities designed to stimulate these areas, such as doing puzzles.

101. **Mindfulness-based therapy**: This kind of therapy teaches individuals to be present and aware of the moment. It can be helpful for individuals with anxiety, stress, or emotional regulation. Mindfulness therapy helps individuals learn to focus on the present moment and cultivate a non-judgmental awareness of their thoughts, feelings, and bodily sensations.

    Mindfulness-based therapy can help improve emotional regulation by providing tools to identify and manage difficult emotions. In addition, mindfulness-based therapy can help improve cognitive skills, such as attention and memory, by practicing exercises that require sustained attention and concentration. It can help your child reduce stress and anxiety by teaching techniques to manage stressors and promote relaxation.

Accessing therapies for your child has many benefits for their overall development and well-being. Treatments can help children improve their social

Supplementary Therapies

skills, academic performance, mental health, confidence, and general quality of life by providing specialized support and instruction.

Please remember to consult healthcare providers before embarking on complementary therapy. You should also be cautious of treatments that make unrealistic claims or promise a "cure." Once you have decided to pursue a particular course of action, you should assess potential risks and monitor progress closely.

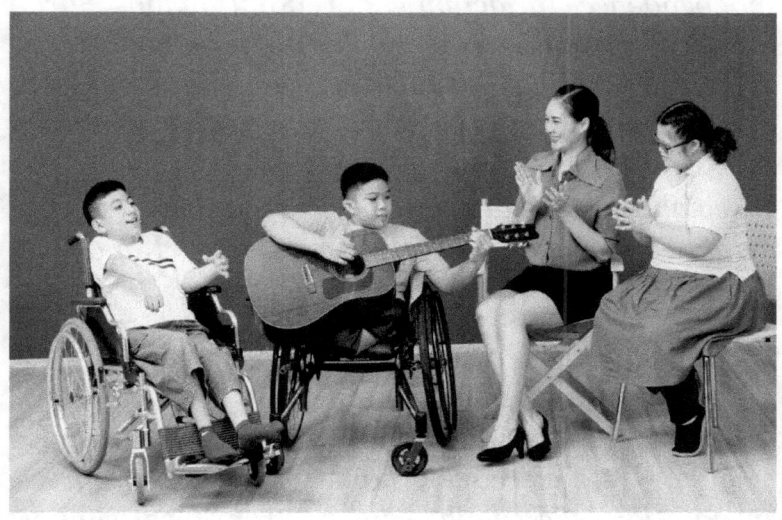

Case Study

Alan is a nine-year-old boy with special needs, significant cognitive delays, and communication impairments. Although he was already accessing occupational, speech, and physiotherapy, his mother,

Sarah, was determined to find complementary therapies to help him thrive.

Recognizing the importance of addressing challenging behaviors and fostering appropriate social interactions, Sarah enrolled Alan in a behavioral therapy program. This evidence-based intervention focused on reinforcing positive behaviors and providing strategies to manage and modify negative behaviors.

To enhance Alan's social skills and improve independence in activities of daily living, Sarah enrolled Alan in a social club aimed at building social skills and learning life skills. As a result, his confidence grew leaps and bounds, and the increased interactions enhanced his speech. The club was especially beneficial since it offered a wide range of activities, including dancing and opportunities to participate in outdoor physical activities.

Sarah actively participated in all aspects of the interventions. She collaborated with facilitators, attended sessions, and implemented recommended strategies and exercises at home to reinforce progress. In addition, she sought support from local support groups and connected with other parents facing similar challenges. This network provided emotional support, guidance, and a platform for sharing experiences and resources.

Alan's participation in the combined therapies yielded significant improvements for several months. Sarah *observed substantial progress in Alan's behavior management, fine motor skills, and communication abilities. Moreover, Alan exhibited increased social interaction, reduced challenging behaviors, and improved speech articulation, allowing for better integration within educational and social settings. Sarah now collaborates with Alan's school and community event organizers to access supplementary interventions for Alan.*

Conclusion

In this book, we have considered the classic definition of Special Needs—limits on a person's intellectual functioning and adaptive behavior. We learned that people with special needs have varying restrictions on their ability to learn and function effectively in society, and they often learn more slowly than others. But with proper support and treatment, most people with special needs maintain successful, productive roles in their communities.

Raising your special child may be challenging, but with the right level of support, it can also be a gratifying and enriching experience filled with love, growth, and joy. Parents play a crucial role in promoting their children's physical health, emotional well-being, education, and personal development. They are perfectly positioned to encourage their children's independence, socialization, communication, and adoption of life skills. In addition, parents can help their children overcome obstacles and achieve their dreams with dedication, patience, and love.

Conclusion

Community involvement and resources can further enhance these efforts, providing a broader support network and specialized services to help our children thrive. By working together as families, communities, and society, we can promote greater understanding, inclusivity, and opportunity for individuals with special needs and ensure they can lead happy, healthy, and fulfilling lives.

Everyone can promote awareness and acceptance of special needs, reduce stigma, and encourage inclusivity. This can involve advocating for policies and laws that protect the rights and dignity of individuals with special needs and promoting better representation and visibility of people with special needs in media and public life.

In addition to the wide-ranging role that parents play in raising their special children, parents should also focus on self-care by accessing support networks and resources to manage stress. This includes seeking counseling or therapy, participating in support groups, or taking time for self-care activities that promote physical and emotional well-being. Seek help from extended family, neighbors, and friends who can provide emotional support. Finally, allocate time to look after yourself to be mentally and physically healthy and strong enough to care for your child.

Depending on where you live, various resources may be available to help you—support groups, advocacy organizations, and government programs. Do what you can to access help, and know that with patience, perseverance, and love, you and your child will thrive together.

Recognize that each child has unique strengths and individual needs. Work closely with your child's healthcare team, educators, and other professionals to develop a personalized care plan and support that addresses their needs and goals. Then, with the proper support, resources, and a commitment to inclusivity and understanding, you can be sure that your child can grow and learn regardless of their disability.

People with mild special needs can learn to care for themselves once they receive the appropriate training. As adults, they often enjoy independence in their daily lives, and many are employed. Those with moderate to high levels of special needs will have much more significant challenges with speech, coordination, and cognition. They also frequently have physical disabilities and may need constant care and supervision. However, most individuals with special needs learn to function better over time.

Early, ongoing interventions can improve functioning, and irrespec-tive of their level of disability, each person can learn and make meaningful contributions to society. They need help and therapies that parents and wider families, caregivers, educators, and the community can collectively provide.

Conclusion

As we conclude this conversation, I'd like to remind you, from one special parent to another, to concentrate on the strengths and abilities of your child and not on their limitations. Actively seek opportunities for your child to learn, grow, and develop independence. Join others to advocate for the rights and well-being of people with special needs everywhere.

By being intentional about our resolve to improve our children's lives, we can create a more inclusive, empathetic, and supportive environment for them to thrive, grow, and play their part in society.

Sometimes all you have to do is be.

—Andrea Campbell

Please leave a review

As an independent author, reviews are very important to me. I'd really appreciate it if you would leave me a review by following the link below or scanning the QR code.

https://www.amazon.com/dp/B0CBNNBRXV

A gift for you

Finding sources of funding and support can pose a real challenge to parents of children with special needs. I've compiled a list of sources where you can find grants, funding, and other support for your special child.

If you'd like a copy, please visit the following link or scan the QR code to download it and subscribe to my newsletter for periodic updates, copies of my books, and other materials.

https://subscribepage.io/Pocket_Learner

About the author

Andrea Campbell, MBA, MA, is a social entrepreneur, linguist, and author. Since publishing her first book in 2010, Andrea has released several inspirational, special needs, business and cultural books. Over the years, she has focused on empowering vulnerable people through education and inspiration.

As the mother of a child with special educational needs, she is particularly keen on working with families to enable their disabled children to aspire higher and achieve their potential. She is also the inventor of the Pocket Learner–a set of innovative educational resources for parents, caregivers, and educators of children with special educational needs.

Andrea has also published a range of inspirational coloring books, journals, and activity books to empower people everywhere. She resides with her family in London, UK, where she continues to make a positive impact through her writing, creative exploits, training programs, coaching, philanthropy, and inspirational speaking.

Other Books by the Author

Special Needs Education: The Pocket Learner

Paperback | Ebook | Hardcover | Audiobook

The Ultimate Toolkit for Every Parent and Caregiver of a Child or Adult with Special Educational Needs and Disabilities

BLENDED FAMILY - A Guide for Stepparents

Paperback | Ebook | Hardcover | Audiobook

Seven Unsuspecting Attitudes That Are Seriously Toxic to Stepfamilies

The Blended Family Parenting Kids with Special Needs
Nine Keys for Building a Happy Stepfamily Caring for Children with Special Needs and Disabilities

Ebook | Audiobook

Blended and Special
Nine Keys for Building a Happy Stepfamily Caring for a Child with Special Needs and Disabilities

Paperback | Hardcover

These two books have the same content.

Resources

Cfp, T. F. D. M. (2022). Physiotherapy vs Physical Therapy: What's the Difference? PTProgress | Career Development, Education, Health. https://www.ptprogress.com/physiotherapy-vs-physical-therapy-whats-the-difference

Garcia, L., & Garcia, L. (2021). Special needs: Defining and understanding the 4 types. Care.com Resources. https://www.care.com/c/types-of-special-needs/

Health and Care of People with Learning Disabilities Experimental Statistics 2020 to 2021 - NDRS. (n.d.). NDRS. https://digital.nhs.uk/data-and-information/publications/ statistical/health-and-care-of-people-with-learning-disabilities/experimental-statistics-2020-to-2021

How common is learning disability? (n.d.). Mencap. https://www.mencap.org.uk/learning-disability-explained/ research-and-statistics/how-common-learning-disability

Huizen, J. (2020, December 2). What to know about intellectual disability. https://www.medicalnewstoday.com/articles/ intellectual-disability#summary

Innocenti, U. O. O. R.-. (n.d.). Research and Evidence on Children with Disabilities : (C)2023 www.unicef-irc.org - UNICEF Office of Research - Innocenti. https://www.unicef-irc.org/children-with-disabilities

Inspirations, N. (2021, August 16). Understanding the Difference Between Autism and Intellectual Disability. I Am Cadence. https://iamcadence.com/2018/03/28/understanding-the-difference-between-autism-and-intellectual-disability/

Libretexts. (2022). 7.2: Sensory Impairments Basic Concepts. Medicine LibreTexts. https://med.libretexts.org/Bookshelves/Nursing/Nursing_Fundamentals_(OpenRN)/07%3A_Sensory_Impairments/7.02%3A_Sensory_Impairments_Basic_Concepts

MEd, J. S. R. (2015, February 16). CHAPTER 4: COMMON PHYSICAL CONCERNS. Pressbooks. https://opentextbc.ca/caregivers/chapter/chapter-four-common-physical-concerns/

O'Handley, R. D., Ford, W. T., Radley, K. C., Helbig, K. A., & Wimberly, J. K. (2016). Social Skills Training for Adolescents With Intellectual Disabilities. Behavior Modification, 40(4), 541–567. https://doi.org/10.1177/0145445516629938

Ohwovoriole, T. (2022). What Is an Intellectual Disability? Verywell Mind. https://www.verywellmind.com/intellectual-disability-definition-symptoms-traits-causes-treatment-5220629

Pathway2success. (2022, July 20). Using Social Scripts for Autism - The Pathway 2 Success. The Pathway 2 Success.

https://www.thepathway2success.com/using-social-scripts-for-autism/

Population Specific Fact Sheet – Intellectual Disability. (n.d.). National Disability Navigator Resource Collaborative. https://nationaldisabilitynavigator.org/ndnrc-materials/fact-sheets/population-specific-fact-sheet-intellectual-disability/

The Scottish Government. (2019). Supporting disabled children, young people and their families: guidance. The Scottish Government. https://www.gov.scot/publications/supporting-disabled-children-young-people-and-their-families/pages/inclusive-communication/

Themwell. (2020, March 11). Special Needs: Common Types, Challenges & Resources - The M Center for Integrative Wellness. The M Center for Integrative Wellness. https://themwellnesscenter.com/special-needs-common-types-challenges-resources/

Website, N. (n.d.). What is autism? nhs.uk. https://www.nhs.uk/conditions/autism/what-is-autism/

What is Intellectual Disability? (n.d.). https://www.psychiatry.org/patients-families/intellectual-disability/what-is-intellectual-disability

www.ingramcontent.com/pod-product-compliance
Lightning Source LLC
Chambersburg PA
CBHW050238120526
44590CB00016B/2138